The
Sacagawea
COOKBOOK

With Contemporary Recipes

ISBN 0-9701378-1-8
Copyright 2001 © by Whisper'n Waters, Inc.
Fourth Printing 2005

Authors: Teri Evenson, Lauren Lesmeister and Jeffrey W. Evenson
Design Director: Elegant Designs, Chelly Bosch, Bismarck, North Dakota
Recipe Editor: Lauren Lesmeister
Copy Editor: Melissa J. Case
Printer: Daehan Printing & Publishing Ltd., Korea
Publishers: Whisper'n Waters, Inc., Bismarck, North Dakota

Front Cover: *"Starting the Fire - Sacagawea and Pomp,"* Original watercolor painting by Michael Haynes, ©2001.

Inside Front Cover: *"Meriwether Lewis"* by Charles Wilson Peale, 1807, Oil on wood panel. *"William Clark,"* by Charles Wilson Peale, 1810, oil on paper. Courtesy of the Independence National Historical Park Collection, National Park Service, 313 Walnut Street, Philadelphia, Pennsylvania. [19106]

Back Cover: Charles Wimar's *"Indians Encampment on the Big Bend of the Missouri River."* 1860, Oil on canvas, 25" X 49", from the collection of Gilcrease Museum, Tulsa, Oklahoma. [0126.1598]

Inside of Back Cover: Charles M. Russell, *"In the Wake of the Buffalo Runner,"* 1911, 29 1/2" X 35 1/2", Photomechanical reproduction, Samuels Collection, Charles M. Russell Center, School of Art, University of Oklahoma, Norman, Oklahoma.

Dedications

To people whose hearts are light and purpose is strong, who take joy in the doing and satisfaction from doing the best they can with what they've got.

Teri Evenson

For Mom, Dad, and Jacqueline. Rest Easy. Wheel turning...

L.L.

To Little Joe,

I have yet to equal my Mother's fire and her tenacity.

One day we were working cattle down in the corrals. It was weaning time. A gentleman from out east arrived and was leaning on the corral. Suddenly he pointed to the ranch hand, way across the corrals, who had just expertly separated a cow/calf pair. "Who's that ranch hand over there?" he asked. It took only a moment and I proudly said, "That's my Mom."

Jeff Evenson

Table of Contents

Acknowledgements for Internal Art Works and Quotes

<u>Front Cover:</u> *"Starting the Fire - Sacagawea and Pomp,"*
An original watercolor painting by Michael Haynes ©2001, Wildwood, Missouri.

<u>Page</u>   <u>Artist</u>   <u>Work</u>

The following works courtesy of Joslyn Art Museum, Omaha, Nebraska.

10   Alfred Jacob Miller   *"The Trapper's Bride,"* Oil on canvas, 30" X 25"
      American, (1810-1874)

The following works are from the collection of Gilcrease Museum, Tulsa, Oklahoma.

21   William Jacob Hayes   *"A Herd of Buffalo on the Bed of the River Missouri,"* 1860,
                                       Oil on Canvas, 36" X 72" [0137.533]

80   Charles M. Russell   *"Lewis and Clark Expedition,"* 1918, Oil on canvas,
      (1846-1926), American   30 1/2" X 48 1/2" [0137.2267]

99   Thomas Moran   *"Shoshone Falls on the Snake River,"* 1900,
      (1837-1926), American   Oil on canvas, 71" X 132" [0126.2339]
      born in England

IBC   Charles Wimar   *"Indians Encampment on the Big Bend of the Missouri River."* 1860,
                                       Oil on canvas, 25" X 49" [0126.1598]

The following works courtesy of Amon Carter Museum, Fort Worth, Texas.

22   Carl Wilmar   *"Indian Crossing the Upper Missouri,"* Oil on canvas [1971.61]
      (ca.1859-1960)

135   Charles M. Russell   *"Lewis and Clark on the Lower Columbia,"* 1905, Opaque and transparent
                                       watercolor over graphite underdrawing on paper, 18 7/8" X 23 7/8"
                                       [1961.195]

171   John Mix Stanley   *"Scene on the Columbia River,"* ca. 1852, Oil on canvas,
                                       17 1/8" X 21 1/8" [1972.45]

185   Charles M. Russell   *"Sun Worship in Montana,"* 1907, Opaque and transparent watercolor over
                                       graphite underdrawing on paper, 22 3/8" X 17 1/2" [1961.150]

The following work is courtesy of the Sid Richardson Collection of Western Art, Fort Worth, Texas.

39   Charles M. Russell   *"Bringing up the Trail,"* 1895, Oil on canvas, 22 7/8" X 35"

The following work is courtesy of the CM Russell Museum, Great Falls, Montana.

40   Charles M. Russell   *"The Beauty Parlor,"* 1907, Watercolor, 8" X 9 3/4"

The following work is courtesy the Buffalo Bill Historical Center, Cody, Wyoming.

59   Henry Farny   *"Days of Long Ago,"* Oil on Board, 37 1/2" X 23 3/4", 6.75
      (1847-1916)

Acknowledgements for Internal Art Works and Quotes (continued)

The following works are courtesy of Mrs. John F. Clymer and the Clymer Museum of Art, Ellensburg, Washington

60	John F. Clymer	*"Lewis and Clark in the Bitterroots,"* 1967, Oil
100	John F. Clymer	*"Angry River,"* 1978, Oil
154	John F. Clymer	*"Visitors at Fort Clatsop,"* 1978, Oil
172	John F. Clymer	*"Sacajawea by the Big Water,"* 1974, Oil
181	John F. Clymer	*"Arrival of Sergeant Pryor,"* 1975, Oil
182	John F. Clymer	*"Captain Clark Gangue of Buffalo,"* 1976, Oil

The following work is courtesy of The Detroit Institute of Arts, A Gift of Dexter M. Ferry, Jr., Detroit Michigan.

79	John Mix Stanley	*"Western Landscape,"* c. 1847/1849, Photograph ©1984

The following works are courtesy of The Stark Museum of Art, Orange, Texas.

117	Paul Kane (1810-1871)	*"A Sangey's Village on the Esquimalt,"* 1847, Watercolor on paper, 5 1/4" X 8 7/8" [31.78/66, WWC 66]
118	Paul Kane (1810-1871)	*"Medicine Masks of the Northwest Coast Tribes,"* 1847, Watercolor on paper 5 1/2" X 8 3/4" [31.78/27, WWC27]
136	Paul Kane (1810-1871)	*"Drying Salmon at the Dalles, Columbia River,"* Watercolor on paper, 5 1/2" X 9 1/4" [31.78/50, WWC 50]
153	Paul Kane (1810-1871)	*"A Chinook Traveling Lodge with View of Mount Hood,"* 1847, Watercolor on paper, 5 1/2" X 9" [31.78/100, WWC 101]

The following work is courtesy of Charles M. Russell Center, Samuels Collection, School of Art, University of Oklahoma, Norman, Oklahoma.

BC	Charles M. Russell	*"In the Wake of the Buffalo Runner,"* 1911, 29 1/2" X 35 1/2" Photomechanical reproduction, Samuels Collection

The Historical Quotes

From the University of Nebraska Press edition of the *Journals of the Lewis and Clark Expedition* edited by Gary Moulton. Used by permission of the University of Nebraska Press. *The Journals of the Lewis and Clark Expedition* are available from the University of Nebraska Press at 800.526.2617 and on the web at nebraskapress.unl.edu.

Quotes from the original Lewis and Clark Journals courtesy of the American Philosophical Society, Philadelphia Pennsylvania.

Quotes from the original Joseph Whitehouse's Journals courtesy of Edward E. Ayer Collection, the Newberry Library, Chicago, Illinois.

Sacagawea

Introduction

We write this book in the spirit of remembrance and gratitude for a woman called by many names, claimed by many tribes, and the inspiration for so many stories. We have incorporated some of the same plants, roots and meats that were available to her into contemporary recipes. We combed the journals of the Corps of Discovery for references to Sacagawea and placed them throughout this book. The art depicts scenes of the Corps' journey, as well as scenes from Indian life as it was likely to have been so long ago.

Sacagawea teaches us to make the very best of our situations. As a tribute to this heroic woman, we have compiled this collection of recipes with many familiar flavors, yet as diverse as the tribes the Corps of Discovery met along the way. We did not restrict our recipes to the ingredients and methods Sacagawea would have used; but embellished them with today's flavors and styles.

Sacagawea walks through the mists of time, babe on back, pointing to a familiar landmark. She beckons us to retrace her steps and witness some of the sights and tastes that she experienced along the way. Journey with us now to the scenes, impressions and tastes that await your adventuresome spirit. Explore the flavors and the dishes we have journaled on our trip down the trail of discovery.

Teri-Ann Evenson

Starting the Fire - Sacagawea and Pomp

An Original Watercolor Painting By: *Michael Haynes*

This painting depicts Sacagawea and her son Jean Baptiste Charbonneau, nicknamed "Pomp," by William Clark, starting a cookfire. This scene explores how Sacagawea might have appeared not long after the Lewis and Clark Expedition. She has just started a small fire which will be allowed to burn down to coals for cooking. In preparation for cooking she has laid out a wooden bowl with maize and perhaps some chokecherries next to her burden basket woven of bark on a willow frame. A well-used copper kettle, of a type common to the early fur trade, stands ready behind the bowl.

Sacagawea has on a very plain, two-hide dress made of elk hide. This early plains pattern was widely adopted at the time by many tribes after replacing the older, side seam dress. Her belt and moccasins are decorated more elaborately with quill and beadwork in traditional Hidatsa patterns. The dyes used by the Hidatsa in their quillwork allowed for some intense and unusual colors. Blue beads were extremely popular and therefore valuable. Sacagawea's jewelry selection for this day is very simple with shell earings and trade metal bracelets and rings. Her braids are bound with strips of red tradecloth and vermillion has been applied to the part in her hair. I've attempted to portray Sacagawea as she may have dressed for a typical day's labor.

July 24, 2001

Michael Haynes

"Starting the Fire - Sacagawea and Pomp"
An original watercolor painting by Michael Haynes, © 2001.

"The Trapper's Bride"
Alfred Jacob Miller (1810-1874), American — 1850, Oil on canvas, 30" X 25"
Courtesy of Josyln Art Museum, Omaha, Nebraska

Soups

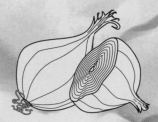

11th February Monday 1805

about five oclock this evening one of the wives of Charbono was delivered of a fine boy. it is worthy of remark that this was the first child which this woman had boarn and as is common in such cases her labour was tedious and the pain violent; Mr. Jessome informed me that he had freequently administered a small portion of the rattle of the rattle-snake, which he assured me had never failed to produce the desired effect, that of hastening the birth of the child; having the rattle of a snake by me I gave it to him and he administered two rings of it to the woman broken in small pieces with the fingers and added to a small quantity of water. Whether this medicine was truly the cause or not I shall not undertake to determine, but I was informed that she had not taken it more than ten minutes before she brought forth perhaps this remedy may be worthy of future experiments, but I must confess that I want faith as to it's efficacy.--

Meriwether Lewis

11

Buffalo Cheese Burger Soup

1 Tablespoon canola oil

1 pound ground buffalo (substitute beef)

1 cup onion, diced

1 cup celery, chopped

2 Tablespoons sun-dried tomatoes in oil, small dice

1 teaspoon dried basil leaves

3/4 teaspoon salt

3 cups chicken broth

1/2 cup sour cream

8 ounces American cheese, cubed

Brown buffalo with onion, celery and sun-dried tomatoes in oil in a Dutch oven over medium heat. Add basil, salt and broth. Stir in sour cream and cheese. Reduce heat and allow cheese to melt. Do not allow soup to boil after adding cheese.

Serve with toasted garlic bread or croutons.

Serves 4

1804

4th of Novr. a french man by Name Chabonah, who Speaks the Big Belley language visit us, he wished to hire & informed us his 2 Squars were Snake Indians, we engau him to go on with us and take one of his wives to interpet the Snake language

William Clark

Charbonneau's Onion Soup

2 Tablespoons butter

1 1/2 teaspoons minced roasted garlic

2 large white onions, medium dice

5 scallions

6 cups beef broth

1/2 teaspoon fresh ground black pepper

1 teaspoon Worcestershire Sauce

1/2 teaspoon ground nutmeg

1/4 teaspoon liquid smoke

1 cup sourdough croutons

6 ounces Gruyere cheese, grated

Place butter, garlic, diced onion, and scallions in a large skillet. Sauté over medium heat until onion is translucent. Transfer to a large soup pot. Add broth, black pepper, Worcestershire sauce, and nutmeg. Bring to a rolling boil. Add liquid smoke. Reduce heat and simmer for one hour. Place croutons in ovenproof bowls. Ladle soup over croutons and top with grated cheese. Place under broiler for 5 minutes or until cheese is brown.

Serve hot.

Serves 4-6

Feb 12th, 1805

On the 12th we arrived at the fort; and found one of our interpreter's wives had in our absence made an addition to our number. [6]

[6] Jean Baptiste Charbonneau was born on February 11, 1805.

Patrick Gass

13

Old Fashioned Vegetable Soup

1 meaty soup bone (elk, buffalo or beef)

1 teaspoon salt

2 quarts water

1 whole dried bay leaf

1 Tablespoon canola oil

1 medium white onion, diced

1 stalk of celery, sliced

2 carrots, sliced

2 potatoes, peeled, large dice

1 quart tomato juice

1 14 1/2-ounce can green beans, drained

1 1/2 cups shredded cabbage

fresh ground black pepper to taste

In a large Dutch oven over medium high heat, boil the soup bone in water along with salt and the bay leaf. Reduce heat and simmer for at least an hour. Remove soup bone from water and place in an ovenproof casserole. Bake in oven at 350 degrees F. for approximately 45 minutes (No need to preheat). In a skillet sauté onion, celery and carrots in oil until onion is translucent and carrots are bright orange. Add mixture to the soup broth, then add potatoes and continue to simmer until carrots and potatoes are almost tender. Add tomato juice, beans and cabbage and continue to simmer. Remove soup bone from oven. Allow bone to cool slightly and then remove the meat from the bones. Add meat to soup. When cabbage is tender, adjust the seasonings to your preference.

Serve with cream.

Serves 8

Old Mandan Bean Soup

1 Tablespoon butter

1 medium onion, chopped

1 carrot, peeled and sliced

1 stalk celery, chopped

several mushrooms (white or button are fine), chopped

1/4 cup sweet corn kernels

1 teaspoon curry powder

2 cups chicken stock

1 medium potato, peeled and cubed

1/4 cup frozen spinach, thawed and drained

1 15 1/2-ounce can great northern beans, drained

1/4 teaspoon ground mace

1/4 teaspoon ground red pepper

1/2 cup light cream

dash of fresh ground black pepper

In large soup pot, sauté onion, carrot, celery, mushrooms and corn with butter until onions are translucent. Add curry powder and sauté another few minutes. Add the chicken stock and potato. Simmer for 20 minutes or until potatoes and carrots are done. Add the rest of the ingredients and simmer an additional 10 minutes. Stir in cream and serve. Add fresh ground black pepper to taste.

Serves 4

Tuesday 9th, Feb 1805

On the 9th we built a pen, to secure our meat from the wolves, which are very numerous here;

Patrick Gass

Cheyenne Chowder

1 Tablespoon canola oil

1 pound smoked ring sausage, sliced

1 red onion, chopped

1/2 cup red bell pepper, diced

1/2 cup green bell pepper, diced

2 carrots, peeled and sliced

4 cups chicken broth

2 cups corn kernels

2 small potatoes, peeled and cubed

1 cup butternut squash, seeded, peeled and diced

1 cup cooked wild rice

2 teaspoons prepared yellow mustard

1/2 teaspoon dried thyme leaves

1/2 cup cream

Garnish:

3-4 slices bacon, browned and crumbled

3-4 teaspoons blue cheese, crumbled

1 teaspoon chopped fresh chives

In a large Dutch oven, lightly brown the sliced sausage in oil. Drain sausage. Add the onion and peppers. Sauté until onion is translucent. Add all ingredients except thyme and cream. Simmer until vegetables are tender. Add cream and thyme. Do not boil soup after adding cream.

Garnish with crisp crumbled bacon, chives and crumbled blue cheese.

Serves 4-6

Ham and Wild Rice Soup

1 large ham bone

2 quarts water

1/2 cup carrots, sliced

1 teaspoon extra virgin olive oil

1/2 large red onion, diced

1/2 cup broccoli, small florets

1/2 cup sweet corn kernels

1 cup cooked wild rice

1/2 teaspoon dried oregano leaves

1/4 teaspoon fresh ground black pepper

1 cup cream

12 ounces American cheese, cubed

1/4 teaspoon liquid smoke

1/4 cup fresh parsley, chopped

Place water and ham bone in a large soup pot. Bring to a rolling boil, reduce heat and simmer for one hour stirring occasionally. Remove bone from soup stock and cool. Remove meat from bone and cut into small pieces. Return meat to the stock. In a separate pan, sauté onion, broccoli and corn in olive oil until onion is translucent. Add onion mixture, rice and spices to soup and simmer for 15 minutes. Add the cream and cheese to the soup mixture and simmer, stirring frequently until cheese is melted. Do not allow mixture to boil. Stir in liquid smoke and serve.

Garnish with fresh chopped parsley.

Serves 4-6

Forest Mushroom Soup

3 ounces fresh shiitake mushrooms, diced

2 medium portabella mushrooms, diced

2 teaspoons roasted garlic, minced

3 scallions, minced

1 large onion, diced

1 Tablespoon canola oil

3 cups chicken stock

2 cups heavy cream

In a large Dutch oven sauté mushrooms, garlic and onions in oil stirring constantly until tender. Add stock. Allow to cool. Blend in food processor until smooth. Return to kettle and add cream with heat on medium. Do not boil. Reduce gently until soup is thick and creamy.

Serves 6

Sunday 20th Jany. 1805

Some men went up to the villages. they informed us that they all used them verry well. gave them pleanty to eat, & when they had done eating they gave a bowl of victuls to a buflows head which they worshiped, & Sd. Eat this So that the live ones may come in that we may git a Supply of meat.

Joseph Whitehouse

Little Bird Soup

1 Tablespoon butter

1/3 cup onion, chopped

2 scallions, sliced

1 teaspoon minced garlic

1 carrot peeled and sliced

2 mushrooms, diced

1 large chicken breast, chopped

6 cups chicken stock

2/3 cup cooked wild rice

1/2 teaspoon dry poultry seasoning

1/4 teaspoon fresh grated ginger root

In a large skillet, sauté onions, garlic, carrot, mushrooms and poultry breast in butter until onions are translucent. In large stock pot, combine stock, rice, seasonings and sautéed ingredients. Simmer for 30 minutes.

Yield: 9-10 cups

6th of March Wednesday 1805

A Cloudy morning & Smokey all Day from the burning of the plains, which was Set on fire by the Minetarries for an early crop of Grass as an endusement for the Buffalow to feed on--

William Clark

29th August 1806

I assended to the high Country and from an eminance, I had a view of the plains for a great distance. from this eminance I had a view of a greater number of buffalow than I had ever Seen before at one time. I must have Seen near 20,000 of those animals feeding on this plain. I have observed that in the country between the nations which are at war with each other the greatest numbers of wild animals are to be found

William Clark

"A Herd of Buffalo on the Bed of the River Missouri"
William Jacob Hayes — 1860, Oil on Canvas, 36" X 72"
From the collection of Gilcrease Museum, Tulsa Oklahoma

"Indian Crossing the Upper Missouri"
Carl Wimar — ca. 1859-1960, Oil on canvas
Courtesy of Amon Carter Museum, Fort Worth, Texas

Fritters and Finger Food

11th of March Monday 1805

We have every reason to believe that our Menetarre interpeter, (whome we intended to take with his wife, as an interpeter through his wife to the Snake Indians of which nation She is) has been Corupted by the {blank} Companeys &c. Some explenation has taken place which Clearly proves to us the fact, we give him to night to reflect and deturmin whether or not he intends to go with us under the regulations Stated.

William Clark

Spinach Dip

1 10-ounce package chopped spinach, thawed and well drained

1 Tablespoon sun-dried tomatoes, chopped

1 clove garlic, minced

1 Tablespoon onions, minced

1/3 cup mayonnaise

1/3 cup sour cream

1 Tablespoon fresh lemon juice

fresh ground black pepper to taste

In a medium bowl, combine ingredients. Cover bowl with plastic food wrap. Refrigerate for several hours.

Serve with crackers or chips.

Yield: about 1 1/2 cups

1805 March 12th

... our Interpeter Shabonah, detumins on not proceeding with us as an interpeter under the terms mentioned yesterday   he will not agree to work let our Situation be what it may not Stand a guard, and if miffed with any man he wishes to return when he pleases, also have the disposial of as much provisions as he Chuses to Carrye.

William Clark

Tree Stick Jerky

3 pounds venison cut in thin strips
   (substitute lean beef or elk)

2 Tablespoons liquid smoke

1/4 cup soy sauce

several dashes pepper sauce

1 Tablespoon Worcestershire sauce

3 Tablespoons maple syrup

1 Tablespoon prepared mustard

1 Tablespoon fresh ground black
   pepper

1 Tablespoon seafood seasoning

1 teaspoon minced garlic

Combine all ingredients in a sealable plastic bag. Refrigerate overnight. Spread strips on a dehydrator rack or in the oven at 200 degrees F. and dry to desired consistency.

Yield: about 1 1/2 pounds of jerky

17th of March Sunday
Mr. Chabonah Sent a french man of our party that he was Sorry for the foolissh part he had acted and if we pleased he would accompany us agreeabley to the terms we had perposed and doe every thing we wished him to doe &c.&c.

William Clark

Sweet Carrot Balls

3 ounces cream cheese, softened

1 teaspoon honey

1/2 cup Colby Jack cheese, shredded

1 cup sweet carrots, shredded and drained

1 teaspoon fresh cilantro, chopped

1/2 teaspoon beau monde seasoning

1/3 cup sunflower nuts, salted and roasted, chopped

In a medium bowl, combine cream cheese, honey, Colby Jack cheese, carrots, cilantro and beau monde. Chill slightly and shape into balls the size of a walnut. Press one side of each ball into the sunflower nuts.

Serve with crackers.

Serves 4-6

18th of March 1805

I am informed of a Party of Christanoes & assinniboins being killed by the Sioux, 50 in Number near the Estableishments on the assinniboin R. a fiew days ago (the effect of Mr. Cammeron, revenge on the Chipaway for Killing 3 of his men) Mr. Tousent Chabono, Enlisted as an Interpreter this evening...

William Clark

Hazelnut Mushroom Pate'

2 Tablespoons butter

2 cloves roasted garlic, minced

1 1/2 cups fresh mushrooms, diced

1 small white onion, small dice

1 cup hazelnuts, chopped

1 Tablespoon basil pesto

1 Tablespoon soy sauce

1 Tablespoon lemon juice

fresh ground black pepper to taste

2 Tablespoons cream cheese

Melt butter in a heavy skillet over medium heat. Add garlic, mushrooms and onion. Sauté until onion is translucent but not yet browned. Transfer to a food processor and add remaining ingredients, except for cream cheese. Process until smooth, add cream cheese and process only until cream cheese is incorporated and mixture is smooth and creamy.

Serve warm or chilled as an appetizer on sourdough bread or unsalted crackers.

Yield: 2 cups

Bitterroot Elk Jerky

1 1/2 pounds elk, cut in thin strips
   (substitute lean beef or venison)

1 1/2 Tablespoons maple syrup

1 1/2 teaspoons kosher salt

1 chipotle pepper, finely chopped

1 Tablespoon apple cider vinegar

2 Tablespoons canola oil

1/2 teaspoon paprika

1/2 teaspoon fresh ground black pepper

1/4 teaspoon liquid smoke

Combine all ingredients in a sealable plastic bag. Refrigerate overnight. Spread strips on a dehydrator rack or in the oven at 200 degrees F. and dry to desired consistency.

Yield: about 3/4 pound

Fort Mandan April 7th 1805

The party are in excellent health and sperits, zealously attatched to the enterprise, and anxious to proceed; not a whisper of murmur or discontent to be heard among them, but all act in unison, and with the most perfect harmony. I took an early supper this evening and went to bed. Capt. Clark myself the two Interpretters and the woman and child sleep in a tent of dressed skins. this tent is in the Indian stile, formed of a number of dressed Buffaloe skins sewed together with sinues.

Meriwether Lewis

Bird Woman's Balsamic Deviled Eggs

8 hard boiled eggs

2 Tablespoons mayonnaise

2 teaspoons prepared mustard

1 teaspoon white balsamic vinegar

1/2 teaspoon granulated white sugar

dash salt

1/4 teaspoon ground paprika

Boil eggs for twenty minutes. Allow to cool in cold water. Peel eggs and cut in half lengthwise. Place yolks in small bowl. Place whites on platter. Mash yolks with fork until crumbly. Stir in remaining ingredients and blend until smooth. Place spoonfuls of yolk mixture in each white half. Sprinkle tops with paprika.

Chill and serve.

Yield: 16 pieces

Monday 8th April, 1805

The woman that is with us is a squaw of the Snake nation of Indians, and wife to our interpreter. We expect she will be of service to us, when passing through that nation. In the afternoon we passed very high bluffs on the South side; one of which had lately been a burning vulcano.

Patrick Gass

Elk Pate'

Version 1:

1 1/2 cups cooked elk, finely shredded

1/2 cup salad dressing

2 cloves roasted garlic, minced

1/4 teaspoon hickory smoked salt

1/2 teaspoon liquid smoke

1 ear pickled baby corn, sliced thin

fresh ground black pepper to taste

Version 2:

1 1/2 cups cooked elk, finely shredded

1/4 cup salad dressing

2 cloves roasted garlic, minced

1/4 cup sweet pickle relish

fresh ground black pepper to taste

kosher salt (optional)

Combine ingredients for each version separately. Allow flavors to blend at least 20 minutes. Served chilled with hard tack (or any hard bread, cracker or toast).

Yield: about 2 cups (each recipe)

Tuesday April 9 1805

"when we halted for dinner the squaw busied herself in serching for the wild artichokes which the mice collect and deposit in large hoards. this operation she performed by penetrating the earth with a sharp stick about some small collections of drift wood. her labour soon proved successful, and she procurrd a good quantity of these roots.

Meriwether Lewis

Turnip Fritters

2 cups cooked mashed turnips

1 Tablespoon melted butter

1/4-1/2 cup sifted white all-purpose flour (as needed)

1/4 cup onion, diced

2 cloves garlic, minced

8 scallions, chopped

1/3 cup sunflower nuts, salted and roasted

2 sticks peppered jerky, diced

1/4 teaspoon ground cayenne pepper

fresh ground black pepper to taste

oil and butter for frying

In a medium mixing bowl, add butter and part of the flour to the turnips. Add the remaining ingredients. The mixture should be just firm enough to hold together, yet not stiff. Add more flour if necessary. Add equal amounts of butter and cooking oil to a heavy skillet over low heat. The fritters should be about 1/2-inch thick and about 2 inches in diameter. When the bottom side is golden brown and crispy, turn fritters carefully and fry until both sides are equally brown and crisp.

Serve hot as an appetizer or as a side with soup or salad.

Yield: 12-15 fritters

Feta Hazelnut Cheese Spread

8 ounces tomato basil Feta cheese, crumbled

4 ounces cream cheese, softened

2 teaspoons extra virgin olive oil

1/4 cup chopped hazelnuts

1/4 cup shredded Colby Jack cheese

1/8 teaspoon minced garlic

Combine the Feta and cream cheese until blended. Add remaining ingredients. Stir until well mixed. Serve on crackers or celery.

Garnish with black olives.

Yield: about 2 cups

Saturday April 13th

...when a suddon squall of wind struck us and turned the perogue so much on the side as to allarm Sharbono who was steering at the time, in this state of alarm he threw the perogue with her side to the wind, when the spritsail gibing was as near overseting the perogue as it was possible to have missed. the wind however abating for an instant I ordered Drewyer to the helm and the sails to be taken in, which was instant executed and the perogue being steered before wind was agin plased in a state of security. this accedent was very near costing us dearly.

Meriwether Lewis

Columbian Salmon Ball

2 cups smoked salmon, flaked

1 8-ounce package cream cheese, softened

1/4 cup salad dressing

1/8 teaspoon ground red cayenne pepper

2 cloves roasted garlic, minced

1 teaspoon fresh ground black pepper

1 teaspoon lemon zest

1 slice garlic toast, crushed

1 Tablespoon Parmesan cheese

Remove and discard skin from salmon. Flake and debone salmon in a medium mixing bowl. In a separate bowl, combine cream cheese with salad dressing, cayenne pepper, garlic, black pepper, and zest. Add salmon and form into a ball. On a separate plate combine toast and Parmesan cheese. Roll ball in mixture until thoroughly covered. Store in refrigerator in covered container overnight to allow the flavors to mingle.

Serve chilled.

Yield: 1 Salmon Ball

Millet and Squash Fritters

1 cup cooked, puréed winter squash
(buttercup, butternut or acorn)

1 cup cooked millet

2 Tablespoons melted butter

1 egg, lightly beaten

1/2 teaspoon hot pepper sauce

1 teaspoon kosher salt

fresh ground black pepper to taste

1 clove garlic, minced

1/3-1/2 cup sifted all-purpose white
flour, as needed

3/4 cup green bell pepper, diced

3/4 cup red onion, diced

4 Tablespoons bacon, crisp fried,
crumbled (optional)

oil for frying

In a mixing bowl, combine millet and squash while both are still warm. Add butter, egg, pepper sauce, salt, pepper and garlic. Stir in flour. Add remaining ingredients and mix lightly. Shape into patties 1/2 inch thick and about 2 1/2 inches in diameter. Fry in hot oil until brown, turn and fry other side until brown.

Serve warm as an appetizer or side dish.

Yield: about 20 fritters

Thursday May 16th

the ballance of our losses consisted of some gardin seeds, a small quantity of gunpowder, and a few culinary articles which fell overboard and sunk, the Indian woman to whom I ascribe equal fortitude and resolution, with any person onboard at the time of the accedent, caught and preserved most of the light articles which were washed overboard...

Meriwether Lewis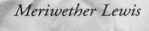

34

Smoky Mushroom Broil

5 slices bacon fried crisp, crumbled

1/4 cup white onion, diced

1 Tablespoon extra virgin olive oil

20 large fresh white mushrooms, stemmed and cored

3/4 cup Ricotta cheese

3/4 cup cream cheese

1 teaspoon dried basil leaves

1 teaspoon sweet Hungarian paprika

1 teaspoon minced roasted garlic

3-4 ounces smoked Gouda cheese, grated fine

Fry the bacon until almost crispy. Remove bacon, drain on a paper towel and crumble. Pour most of the bacon drippings from frying pan. Put the onion and olive oil in the same skillet and sauté until onions are translucent. Return bacon to pan and remove from heat. In a medium bowl, combine cheeses with basil, paprika and garlic. Stir in the onion mixture. Stuff mushrooms with cheese mixture and top with Gouda. Broil until cheese just starts to brown and bubble.

Yield: 20 mushrooms

Shrimp and Potato Fritters

3 cups cooked, mashed potatoes, still warm

1 Tablespoon melted butter

1 egg, lightly beaten

1/4 cup sifted all-purpose white flour

1/2 teaspoon kosher salt

1 Tablespoon seafood seasoning

fresh ground black pepper to taste

1/4 cup red onion, diced

2 scallions, chopped fine

1/2 cup fresh or frozen (blanched) peas

1/2 cup fresh or frozen (blanched) whole kernel corn

1 Tablespoon fresh dill weed, chopped fine

1 pound cooked salad shrimp

butter and corn oil for frying

Combine potatoes, butter and egg. Add flour, salt, seafood seasoning and pepper. Gently fold in onion, scallions, peas, corn and dill. Incorporate shrimp gently with clean, well oiled hands. Shape into patties 1/2-inch thick and about 2 inches in diameter. Place equal parts butter and corn oil in a heavy skillet over low heat and fry patties until crisp and brown, turn and fry other side until crisp and brown.

Serve warm as an appetizer with *Creamy Mustard Sauce* (see recipe page 177).

Yield: about 20 fritters

BBQ Buffalo Nachos

Meat Mixture:

1 pound ground buffalo

1 Tablespoon olive oil

1/2 large onion, chopped

1 cup barbecue sauce (your favorite)

pinch salt

fresh ground black pepper to taste

Layers:

1 15-ounce can black beans, drained

1 Jalapeno pepper, seeded and diced

1 yellow bell pepper, diced

1 tomato, seeded and diced

1/2 cup red onion, diced

5 ounces extra sharp Cheddar cheese, grated

Toppings:

sour cream (as desired)

fresh chopped cilantro (as desired)

baked hard tack wedges (or tortilla chips)

In a Dutch oven over medium heat, brown meat and onions in oil until meat is done. Add BBQ sauce, salt and pepper to meat mixture, reduce heat to low and simmer for 15 minutes. On a large microwaveable platter, layer first the meat mixture, then the layers in the order listed above. Microwave platter until cheese is melted. Remove from microwave and top with sour cream and cilantro.

Serve with hard tack or tortilla chips.

Serves 5-7

Buffalo Bundles

15 pieces frozen bun dough or
    1/2 Sourdough Bread recipe
    (see page 55)

1 pound ground buffalo (substitute
    ground beef)

2 Tablespoons extra virgin olive oil

1/2 cup white onion, fine dice

2 teaspoons minced roasted garlic

3 scallions, diced

1/4 cup hot spicy prepared mustard

1 teaspoon hot pepper sauce

1/4 cup ketchup

3 Tablespoons sun-dried tomatoes in
    oil, chopped

1/8 teaspoon liquid smoke

1 cup portabella mushrooms, fine dice

fresh ground black pepper to taste

1 cup smoked Gouda cheese, shredded

1 egg, gently beaten with 1 Tablespoon
    water

Allow frozen bun dough to rise, or separate sourdough as you would for buns.
Preheat oven to 325 degrees F. In a large frying pan, add meat, oil, onion, garlic
and scallions. Sauté until onions are translucent. Add mustard, pepper sauce,
ketchup and sun-dried tomatoes. Simmer until boiling. Remove from heat and
allow to cool slightly. Stretch and pull pieces of the dough to form an oval. Take
1 heaping tablespoon of meat mixture and place in the middle of each piece of
dough. Pepper to taste. Top with mushrooms and shredded cheese. Moisten
sides of dough and seal shut with a fork forming a half moon. Brush tops with
egg mixture. Place on a greased cookie sheet and bake for 20 minutes or until
golden brown.

Yield: 15 pieces

"Bringing up the Trail"

Charles M. Russell — 1895, Oil on canvas, 22 7/8" X 35"

Courtesy of Sid Richardson Collection of Western Art, Fort Worth, Texas

"The Beauty Parlor"
Charles M. Russell — 1907, Watercolor, 8" X 9 3/4"
Courtesy of C.M. Russell Museum, Great Falls, Montana

Breads and Biscuits

April 1 1805

we have Thunder lightning hail and rain to day   the first rain of note
Sinc the 15 October last, I had the Boat Perogus & Canos put in
the water, and expect to Set off the boat with despatches in her will
go 6 Americans 3 frenchmen, and perhaps Several ricarra Chief
imediately after we Shall assend in 2 perogus & 6 canoes,
accompanied by 5 french who intends to assend a Short distance to
trap the beavr which is in great abundance highr up our party will
consist of one Interpter & Hunter, one French man as an interpreter
with his two wives (this man Speaks Minetary to his wives who are L
hiatars or Snake Indians of the nations through which we Shall
pass, and to act as interpretress thro him [)]-- 26 americans & french
my servant and an Mandan Indian and provisions for 4 months--

William Clark

Sunflower Tomato Biscuits

3 1/4 cups sifted all-purpose white
    flour

1/4 cup corn meal

1 Tablespoon granulated white sugar

2 3/4 teaspoons baking powder

1/4 teaspoon baking soda

1/4 teaspoon dried dill weed

1/2 teaspoon salt

1/4 cup softened butter

1/3 cup roasted sunflower nuts, unsalted

3/4 - 1 cup cold buttermilk, as needed

2 cloves roasted garlic, minced

1/4 teaspoon butter flavoring

1/4 cup sun-dried tomatoes in oil,
    small dice

melted butter as needed

Preheat oven to 325 degrees F. In a bowl, mix flour, cornmeal, sugar, baking powder, baking soda, dill weed and salt. Cut in butter and mix until evenly distributed. Stir in sunflower nuts. Add buttermilk, starting with 1/2 cup. Fold dough gently and do not over mix. Add garlic, butter flavoring and sun-dried tomatoes. Add more buttermilk gradually and when dough forms, stop mixing. Roll dough out on a floured surface, cut out biscuits, transfer to greased baking sheet and brush tops with melted butter. Bake for about 15 minutes, until tops are lightly browned.

Yield: 12-15 biscuits

Creamy Bleu' Berry French Toast

12 slices Sourdough Bread (see recipe page 55)

1 1/3 cups sour cream, divided

1/4 cup heavy cream

1 teaspoon lemon zest

1/8 teaspoon vanilla extract

1 8-ounce package cream cheese

2 Tablespoons granulated white sugar

1/8 teaspoon vanilla extract

2 cups fresh blueberries, divided

1/4 cup melted butter

6 eggs, beaten

1/3 cup whole milk

1/4 teaspoon ground nutmeg

1/8 teaspoon ground mace

1/8 teaspoon ground cinnamon

1/8 teaspoon ground cloves

1/8 teaspoon ground allspice

1/4 cup walnuts, chopped fine

The night before set out bread to dry. Preheat oven to 400 degrees F. Combine the sour cream, heavy cream, zest and vanilla. Set aside. Combine cream cheese, sugar and vanilla. Blend until smooth. Gently fold in 1 cup of blueberries. Place melted butter in 15 1/2x10x1/2-inch jelly roll pan. Set aside. Spread 1 1/2 tablespoons cream cheese mixture between 2 slices of bread. Mix eggs, milk, nutmeg, mace, cinnamon, cloves and allspice. Dip bread into egg mixture to coat sides. (Do it quickly as bread absorbs moisture quickly). Place in buttered pan and bake for 7 minutes on each side. Turn broiler on and broil until tops are golden brown.

Garnish with remaining fresh blueberries and walnuts.

Serve with your favorite syrup.

Yield: 6 servings

Sweet Bread Braid

Day 1
Starter:

1/2 cup *Sourdough Starter* (see recipe page 54)

1/4 teaspoon butter flavoring

1 cup lukewarm water

1 cup sifted all-purpose white flour

Day 2
Bread:

1/2 teaspoon salt

1/4 teaspoon baking powder

1/4 cup granulated white sugar

1 1/2 Tablespoons canola oil

1 egg yolk, slightly beaten

1 teaspoon ground mace

1/2 teaspoon vanilla

1 teaspoon lemon zest

2 1/2-3 cups sifted all-purpose white flour

butter

Streusel:

2 Tablespoons unsalted butter

1/4 cup brown sugar, firmly packed

1/4 cup granulated white sugar

1/2 cup old fashioned oatmeal

1/4 cup chopped pecans

1/4 teaspoon ground mace

1/4 teaspoon ground cinnamon

1/4 teaspoon ground cloves

1/4 teaspoon ground allspice

1/4 teaspoon ground nutmeg

(see next page)

Sweet Bread Braid (continued)

Day 1:
Combine starter, flavoring, water and flour in large bowl. Cover loosely and let stand in a warm place overnight.

Day 2:
Sift salt and baking powder into sourdough mixture. Add sugar, oil, egg yolk, mace, vanilla, lemon zest and 1 cup of sifted flour. Mix well. Add remaining flour as needed. Knead until smooth. Butter top of dough and bottom of bowl. Let stand in a warm place, covered, for 2 hours. For streusel, place butter and sugars in a cast iron skillet. Melt over low heat. Stir mixture until sugar is dissolved. Remove from heat and set aside. Punch dough down after raised double. On a lightly floured surface, shape into 2 cords, each about 18 inches long. Join at one end and tuck under. Braid and tuck remaining end. Let rise in warm place until double (about 1 hour). Put butter/sugar mixture along with the rest of the ingredients for streusel in blender. Blend until coarse in texture. Preheat oven to 375 degrees F. Place braid in oven. Bake for 20 minutes until brown. Remove from oven. Spoon streusel mixture over top of braid and return to oven for an additional 10 minutes (until browned). Allow to cool slightly.

Serve with butter.

Yield: 1 bread braid

Berry Bread

1/2 cup granulated white sugar

2 1/2 cups sifted all-purpose white flour

2 teaspoons baking powder

1 teaspoon baking soda

1 teaspoon ground cinnamon

1/2 teaspoon ground nutmeg

1/2 teaspoon kosher salt

1 teaspoon vanilla extract

1/2 cup canola oil

2 eggs, beaten

1/2 cup buttermilk

1/2 cup maple syrup

1 cup dried sweetened cranberries, diced

Preheat oven to 325 degrees F. In a medium bowl combine dry ingredients. Stir in the rest of the ingredients except for the berries. When well combined, carefully fold in the berries. Divide batter into two 7x4x2-inch loaf pans. Bake for 60 minutes or until a knife inserted in the middle comes out clean.

Serve warm with butter.

Yield: About 8 slices per pan

Thursday April 25th

The dew at this place never falls; and it seldom Rains, this we were told, by an Indian Women that was with us, that embark'd on board one of the Pettyaugers at the Mandan Nation with a frenchman her husband as our Interpreters to the Snake Indians.--

Joseph Whitehouse

Molasses Bread

1 cup warm water

1 1/4 teaspoons yeast

1/4 cup molasses

1 egg, beaten

2 Tablespoons butter

1/2 teaspoon salt

1/2 cup raisins

1/4 cup cornmeal

3 cups sifted all-purpose white flour

In a large mixing bowl, combine water, yeast and molasses. Add the egg, butter, salt, raisins, cornmeal and some of the flour. Keep on adding flour, hand kneading when the dough is too thick to stir. Knead until dough is smooth and satiny. Oil bowl and top of dough. Let rise in warm place until dough doubles in size, 60-90 minutes. Punch down and shape into a loaf and place in a 9x5-inch loaf pan. Preheat oven to 350 degrees F. Allow dough 45-60 minutes to rise or until just about doubled in size. Bake for 60 minutes. Remove from oven and brush top with butter. Cool before cutting.

Yield: 1 loaf

Monday April 29th (1805)

This animal is about the size of a large Buck deer, -the Colour Grey, and has hair coarse & like that of a Goat, it ears small and its body lengthy, the horns like that of a Ram, (sheep) but four times as large. They are very nimble, and generally are to be found on high Mountains and Bluffs, and are very Shy, and difficult to be come at.-- The Indian women that was with us, inform'd us that those animals were very common to be found On the Rocky moutains.--

Joseph Whitehouse

Plain Jane Buns

1 1/4 cups warm milk

1 1/4 teaspoons yeast

1/4 cup granulated white sugar

1 egg, beaten

2 Tablespoons butter

1/2 teaspoon salt

3 1/3 cups sifted all-purpose white flour

In a large mixing bowl combine milk, yeast and sugar until yeast dissolves. Add the egg, butter, salt and some of the flour. Keep adding flour, hand kneading until dough is smooth and satiny. Oil bowl and top of dough. Cover bowl and let rise in warm place until dough doubles in size, about 60-90 minutes. Punch down and shape into buns, place on a baking sheet. Preheat oven to 350 degrees F. Allow buns to rise for 30 minutes or until doubled in size. Bake for 12 minutes. Remove from oven and brush tops with butter.

Yield: 2 dozen rolls

Friday April 26th 1805

after I had completed my observations in the evening I walked down and joined the party at their encampment on the point of land fromed by the junction of the rivers; found them all in good health, and much pleased at having arrived at this long wished for spot, and in order to add in some measure to the general pleasure which seemed to pervade our little community, we ordered a dram to be issued to each person; this soon produced the fiddle, and they spent the evening with much hilarity, singing & dancing, and seemed as perfectly to forget their past toils, as they appeared regardless of those to come.

Meriwether Lewis

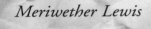

Sunny Corn Biscuits

2 cups sifted all-purpose white flour

1/4 cup yellow cornmeal

1 Tablespoon granulated white sugar

3 1/2 teaspoons baking powder

1/2 teaspoon baking soda

1/4 cup softened butter

3 Tablespoons crushed tortilla chips

3 Tablespoons roasted and salted sunflower nuts

1 cup cold buttermilk, more if needed

melted butter as needed

Preheat oven to 325 degrees F. In a bowl, mix flour, cornmeal, sugar, baking powder and baking soda. Cut in butter and mix until evenly distributed. Stir in crushed chips and sunflower nuts. Add buttermilk, starting with 1/2 cup. Fold dough gently and do not over mix. Add more milk gradually and when dough forms, stop mixing. Roll dough out on a floured surface, cut out biscuits, transfer to baking sheet and brush tops with melted butter. Bake for about 15 minutes, until tops are lightly browned.

Yield: 12-15 biscuits

May the 8th Wednesday 1805
the Countrey on the Lard. Side is high & broken with much Stone Scattered on the hills, In walking on Shore with the Interpreter & his wife, the Squar Geathered on the Sides of the hills wild Lickerish, & the white apple as called by the angegies {engagès} and gave me to eat, the Indians of the Missouri make great use of the white apple dressed in different ways--

William Clark

Fiesta Corn Bread

1 1/4 cups yellow cornmeal

1 1/4 cups sifted all-purpose white flour

4 teaspoons baking powder

3/4 teaspoon kosher salt

1 teaspoon chili powder

2 eggs, lightly beaten

1 cup milk

1 cup cooked pumpkin

2 Tablespoons corn or canola oil

1 1/2 Tablespoons honey

3/4 cup diced green bell pepper

1/3 cup diced red onion

2 cloves garlic, minced

3/4 cup cooked red beans, drained

1 cup grated cheese (Gruyere or Cheddar)

Preheat oven to 325 degrees F. In a bowl, combine cornmeal, flour, baking powder, salt and chili powder. In a separate bowl, combine eggs, milk, pumpkin, oil, and honey. Add wet mixture to dry mixture and mix lightly. Add bell pepper, onion, garlic and beans. Pour batter into an oiled 9x13-inch baking pan and sprinkle the grated cheese evenly over the surface. Bake for 25-30 minutes, or until a knife inserted comes out clean. You may cover the top of the pan with tinfoil during baking.

Serve as a side with your favorite entree.

Yield: 12-15 pieces (depending upon size)

Sourdough Hard Tack

Day 1:

1 cup *Sourdough Starter* (see recipe
   page 54)

1/2 teaspoon butter flavoring

2 cups lukewarm water

2 cups sifted all-purpose white flour

Day 2:

1 teaspoon salt

1/2 teaspoon baking powder

1/2 cup granulated white sugar

3 Tablespoons canola oil

1 egg, slightly beaten

5-6 cups sifted all-purpose white flour

butter

Day 1: Combine starter, flavoring, water and flour in large bowl. Cover loosely and let stand in a warm place overnight.

Day 2: Sift salt and baking powder into sourdough mixture. Add sugar, oil, egg, and 2 cups of sifted flour. Mix well. Add remaining flour as needed, knead until smooth. Butter top of dough and bottom of bowl. Let stand in a warm place, covered, for 2 hours. Punch down and divide into 12 parts. Shape into 12 small round loaves. Place on a lightly floured surface and let rise 1 hour. Preheat oven to 400 degrees F. On a lightly floured surface roll out loaf with a spiked rolling pin. Hard tack should be round and about 1 foot in diameter for baking. To transfer to baking pan, fold dough in half and then in thirds to the center. Transfer to a heavy round pizza pan, place on top rack in oven. While that is baking, roll out another hard tack. When hard tack is rolled out, slip baking hard tack from the top rack to the bottom rack in oven. Place unbaked dough on pizza pan and place on top rack in oven. Roll out next loaf. When rolled out (this should take about 1 1/2 to 2 minutes), it's time to move hard tack on bottom rack to a cooling rack, slip hardtack on pizza pan from top rack to bottom rack and place unbaked dough on pizza pan and place on top rack in oven. Repeat this process until all hard tack is baked.

Yield: 12 hardtack rounds

Rocky Mountain Sweet Rolls

Day 1
Starter:
1/2 cup *Sourdough Starter* (see recipe page 54)

1/4 teaspoon butter flavoring

1 cup lukewarm water

1 cup sifted all-purpose white flour

Day 2
Dough:
1/2 teaspoon salt

1/4 teaspoon baking powder

1/4 cup granulated white sugar

1 1/2 Tablespoons canola oil

1 egg yolk, slightly beaten

1 teaspoon ground mace

1/2 teaspoon vanilla

2 1/2-3 cups sifted all-purpose white flour

Caramel:
1/2 cup butter

1/2 cup brown sugar, firmly packed

1 Tablespoon cream

1/2 cup chopped pecans

Filling:
2 Tablespoons butter

1/2 teaspoon ground cinnamon

2 Tablespoons granulated white sugar

1/4 cup dried currants

(see next page)

Rocky Mountain Sweet Rolls (continued)

<u>Day 1:</u> Combine starter, flavoring, water and flour in large bowl. Cover loosely and let stand in a warm place overnight.

<u>Day 2:</u> Sift salt and baking powder into sourdough mixture. Add sugar, oil, egg yolk, mace, vanilla and 1 cup of sifted flour. Mix well. Add remaining flour as needed. Knead until smooth. Butter top of dough and bottom of bowl. Let stand in a warm place, covered, for 2 hours. For caramel, place butter, brown sugar and cream in a cast iron skillet. Melt over low heat, stirring mixture until sugar is dissolved. Remove from heat and sprinkle nuts evenly over the butter mixture. Punch dough down after raised double. On a lightly floured surface, shape into a rectangle (about 18x12-inches). In a small bowl combine cinnamon and sugar. Spread dough with butter and then sprinkle with cinnamon mixture and currants. Roll up lengthwise and seal long edge. Cut roll in 1 1/2 inch slices. Place roll on nuts in skillet. Let rise 1 hour. Preheat oven to 375 degrees F. Bake for 20 minutes until brown. Remove from oven. Allow pan to cool slightly. Invert to a platter and scrape remaining caramel onto rolls.

Serve with butter.

Yield: 12 rolls

Sourdough Starter

1 package active dry yeast

2 3/4 cups lukewarm water

3 1/4 cups sifted all-purpose white flour

In a medium bowl, dissolve yeast in warm water. Add flour and stir until smooth. Pour starter in large jar and cover loosely for 24 hours. Starter should be bubbly and smell yeasty. Store in refrigerator covered tightly.

For every cup of starter used, add 1 cup flour and 3/4 cup water to the jar. Always leave at least 1 cup of starter in the jar to keep starter active. Each week remove a cup of starter, either for baking or to discard. This will keep the starter fresh.

Wednesday May 29th 1805

I counted the remains of the fires of 126 Indian lodges which appeared to be of very recent date perhaps 12 to 15 days. Capt. Clark also saw a large encampent just above the entrance of this river on the Stard. side of reather older date, probably they were the same Indians. The Indian woman with us exmined the mockersons which we found at these encampments and informed us that they were not of her nation the Snake Indians...

Meriwether Lewis

Sourdough Bread

Day 1:
1 cup *Sourdough Starter* (see recipe
   page 54)
1/2 teaspoon butter flavoring
2 cups lukewarm water
2 cups sifted all-purpose white flour

Day 2:
1 teaspoon salt
1/2 teaspoon baking powder
2 Tablespoons granulated white sugar
3 Tablespoons canola oil
5-6 cups sifted all-purpose white flour
butter

<u>Day 1:</u> Combine starter, flavoring, water and flour in large bowl. Cover loosely and let stand in a warm place overnight.

<u>Day 2:</u> Sift salt and baking powder into sourdough mixture. Add sugar, oil, and 2 cups of sifted flour. Mix well. Add remaining flour as needed. Knead until smooth. Butter top of dough and bottom of bowl. Let stand in a warm place, covered, for 2 hours. Punch down and divide into 2 parts, forming 2 round loaves. Place loaves on oiled baking sheets and set in warm place for 1 hour. Bake at 350 degrees F for 1 hour, until golden brown. Remove from oven and brush tops with butter.

Serve slices warm with butter.

Yield: 2 loaves

Wild Rice Waffles

1 cup sifted all-purpose white flour

1 cup stirred whole wheat flour

1 teaspoon baking soda

1 Tablespoon cornstarch

1 Tablespoon brown sugar, firmly packed

1/2 teaspoon salt

1 3/4 cups buttermilk

2 Tablespoons apple cider vinegar

2 eggs, beaten

1/4 cup canola oil

1 cup cooked wild rice

1 teaspoon vanilla extract

Mix flours, soda, cornstarch, brown sugar and salt in a bowl. Stir in buttermilk, vinegar, eggs, oil, rice and vanilla. Mix until moistened. Mixture will be a little lumpy. Spoon batter onto a hot waffle iron. Close and bake until steaming stops (about 4 minutes).

Yield: 6-7 waffles

Monday June 10th 1805

Sâh-câh-gâh, weâ, our Indian woman is very sick this evening; Capt. C. blead her.

Meriwether Lewis

Pumpkin Corn Bread

1/4 cup white cornmeal

2 cups sifted all-purpose white flour

2 teaspoons baking powder

1/8 teaspoon mace

3 Tablespoons butter

1/4 cup brown sugar, firmly packed

1 cup cooked pumpkin

1/2 cup milk

1 egg, lightly beaten

1 teaspoon vanilla

2 Tablespoons corn oil

Preheat oven to 350 degrees F. In a bowl combine cornmeal, flour, baking powder and mace. In a separate bowl, blend butter, brown sugar, pumpkin, milk, egg, vanilla and corn oil. Add wet mixture to dry and beat until smooth. Pour batter into a 13 X 9-inch oiled baking pan. Bake for about 25 minutes or until a knife inserted comes out clean. Remove from heat and allow 10 minutes to cool.

Serve with butter and honey.

Yield: 15-18 slices depending on size.

June 11th Tuesday 1805

...the Indian woman verry Sick, I blead her which appeared to be of great Service to her...

William Clark

Scallion and Corn Fry Bread

2 cups warm water

1 package dry yeast

1 Tablespoon honey

1 Tablespoon molasses

2 cups sifted all-purpose
white flour

Place water in large mixing bowl, add yeast and dissolve. Add honey and molasses and stir well. Add flour, 1 cup at a time, until a smooth batter is formed. Cover and set in a warm place until doubled in size, about 40-60 minutes.

1/4 cup corn oil

1 teaspoon kosher salt

1 cup yellow cornmeal

2 cups sifted all-purpose
white flour, more as
needed

1/2 cup corn kernels

3 scallions, sliced in
thin diagonals

oil for deep-frying

Stir oil and salt into batter. Add cornmeal and stir until batter is smooth. Add flour, 1/2 cup at a time, until dough is too stiff to mix by hand. Turn dough out onto a floured surface and dust top of dough with a little flour. Allow dough to rest for at least 5-10 minutes. Knead until dough is smooth and elastic, adding flour as necessary. Shape into a ball and place in an oiled bowl. Oil the surface of the dough and cover bowl. Place in a warm spot until doubled in size, about 40-60 minutes. Place dough on a lightly oiled surface and flatten into a large rectangle. Spread corn and scallions over dough, roll up and knead gently. Return dough to oiled bowl and allow dough to rise in a warm place an additional 30 minutes. Cut off small pieces, stretch carefully into rectangles and fry in hot oil, turning once. Drain on paper towels and sprinkle with a little kosher salt.

NOTE: This dough may also be baked as 2 loaves in standard size loaf pans. Use an oven preheated to 325-350 degrees F. for 40-50 minutes.

Serve warm, topped with a little cream cheese or honey.

Yield: 20-30 pieces, depending on size

"Days of Long Ago"
Henry Farny (1847-1916) — Oil on board, 37 1/2" X 23 3/4"
Courtesy of Buffalo Bill Historical Center, Cody, Wyoming, 6.75

"Lewis and Clark in the Bitterroots"
John F. Clymer — 1967, Oil
Courtesy of Clymer Museum & Gallery, Ellensburg, Washington

Greens and Grains

Saturday [NB: Monday] Septr. 16th 1805
...The South <Knobs> Steep hills Side & falling timber Continue to day, and a thickly timbered Countrey of 8 different kinds of pine, which are So covered with Snow, that in passing thro them we are continually covered with Snow, I have been wet and as cold in every part as I ever was in my life, indeed I was at one time fearfull my feet would freeze in the thin mockersons which I wore, after a Short delay in the middle of the Day, I took one man and proceeded on as fast as I could about 6 miles to a Small branch passing to the right, halted and built fires for the party agains their arrival which was at Dusk verry cold and much fatigued we Encamped at this Branch in a thickly timbered bottom which was Scercely large enough for us to lie leavil, men all wet cold and hungary.

William Clark

Spinach Salad

Salad:

1 pound fresh spinach, washed, dried and torn into pieces

3 scallions, sliced thin

2 medium tomatoes, seeded and diced

2 strips jerky, cut into matchsticks

1/2 cup roasted and salted sunflower nuts

1/2 cup dried blueberries

1-2 sprigs fresh dill, minced

Dressing:

1/2 cup extra virgin olive oil

1/4 cup prepared yellow mustard (scant)

2 teaspoons granulated white sugar

2 cloves roasted garlic, minced

fresh ground black pepper to taste

Place all salad ingredients in a large bowl. Whisk all dressing ingredients together in a small bowl. Drizzle dressing over salad immediately before serving and toss lightly.

Serves 4

June 12th 1805 Wednesday
The interpreters wife verry Sick So much So that I move her into the back part of our Covered part of the Perogue which is Cool, her own situation being a verry hot one in the bottom of the <Canoe> Perogue exposed to the Sun–

William Clark

Rice, Bean and Barley Casserole

1 cup cooked red beans

3/4 cups brown rice

1/4 cup barley

1/4 teaspoon kosher salt

1 Tablespoon olive oil

1 medium onion, large dice

1 1/2 cups water

Preheat oven to 325 degrees F. Combine all ingredients in an ovenproof casserole with a lid and bake for approximately 60 minutes. Remove from heat and allow flavors to blend 10-15 minutes.

Serve as a side dish instead of potatoes or rice.

Serves 3-4

June 14th Friday 1805

a fine morning, the Indian woman complaining all night & excessively bad this morning-- her case is Somewhat dangerous--

William Clark

Layered Greens Salad

3 cups iceberg lettuce, chopped

1 cup other greens (cress and dandelion), chopped

1/3 cup onion, chopped

1 carrot, peeled and chopped

1/3 cup jicama (substitute water chestnuts), peeled and cut in matchsticks

1/2 cup mayonnaise

1/4 cup sour cream

1 Tablespoon sugar

1 Tablespoon chili powder

1/2 cup smoked sharp Cheddar cheese, shredded

1/2 cup Canadian bacon (substitute ham), cubed

1/4 cup dried blueberries

1/4 cup unsalted roasted sunflower nuts

Toss greens together on a platter. Next, layer onion, carrot and jicama. In a small bowl combine mayonnaise, sour cream, sugar and chili powder. Pour mayonnaise mixture over salad. Layer the cheese, Canadian bacon, berries and nuts on top.

Serves 6

June the 15th Satturday 1805

...the Indian woman much wors this evening, She will not take any medison, her husband petetions to return &c.

William Clark

Spinach and Cheese Bundles

3 eggs, beaten

3 cloves garlic, minced

1 cup Ricotta cheese

1 cup Parmesan cheese

1/4 cup fresh dill weed, finely chopped

2 Tablespoons fresh cilantro, finely chopped

1 10-ounce package frozen chopped spinach, thawed and drained

2 Tablespoons sun-dried tomatoes in oil, finely chopped

1/2 teaspoon fresh ground black pepper

1/4 teaspoon kosher salt

1 1/2 cups Mozzarella cheese, shredded

1/2 cup melted butter

5 sheets philo dough

Preheat oven to 375 degrees F. Combine eggs, garlic, Ricotta cheese, Parmesan cheese, dill, cilantro, spinach, sun-dried tomatoes, black pepper, salt and Mozzarella in a medium bowl. Place philo dough on wax paper and cover with damp towel. Butter a sheet of philo. Place another sheet of philo on the buttered sheet. Spoon 1/10 mixture along one edge of the sheet. Roll the sheet starting from the edge with the spinach mixture on it. Place on cookie sheet and repeat this procedure with the remaining sheets. Brush bundles with butter and bake for 30 minutes. Cut each bundle into 3 pieces.

Serve warm.

Yield: 15 bundles

Buffalo Cabbage Rolls

1 pound ground buffalo (substitute beef)

1/2 cup onion, chopped

1 Tablespoon Cajun seasoning

1 teaspoon fresh ground black pepper

1 egg, beaten

2 cups cooked white rice

1 cup cooked wild rice

8 large cabbage leaves, steamed

1 8-ounce can tomato sauce

1 Tablespoon apple cider vinegar

butter

additional apple cider vinegar

Combine buffalo, onion, spices, egg and rices. Divide mixture into 8 parts. Wrap each mixture with a cabbage leaf and place in slow cooker. Pour tomato sauce over rolls and add vinegar. Cook on low for 4 hours until done.

Serve with butter and vinegar.

Yield: 8 cabbage rolls

Sunday June 16th 1805

about 2 P.M. I reached the camp found the Indian woman extreemly ill and much reduced by her indisposition. this gave me some concern as well for the poor object herself, then with a young child in her arms, as from the consideration of her being our only dependence for a friendly negociation with the Snake Indians on whom we depend for horses to assist us in our portage from the Missouri to the columbia River.

Meriwether Lewis

Barley and Millet Skillet

Grains:

1 Tablespoon olive oil

3/4 cup quick cooking barley

1/4 cup millet

2 cups chicken stock

Skillet:

1 teaspoon garlic, minced

2 Tablespoons canola oil

1/4 cup slivered carrots

1/4 cup diced onion

1/4 cup diced red bell pepper

1/3 cup small broccoli florets

1/4 cup celery, diced

1/2 teaspoon ground coriander

1/2 cup chopped pecans

fresh ground black pepper to taste

soy sauce to taste

Lightly toast grains in olive oil over medium heat in a skillet until grain turns light brown. Transfer grain to a saucepan with stock. Bring to a boil and then reduce heat to low. Cover and cook for 15 minutes. Remove from heat and let stand 5 minutes. Add oil to skillet along with vegetables. Stir-fry tender crisp. Add grains, spices and nuts. Stir-fry an additional 2-3 minutes. Sprinkle with black pepper and soy sauce, remove from heat and let stand for 5 minutes.

Serves 4-6

Wild Rice Stuffing for Poultry

1/2 cup butter

1 large onion, chopped

1 clove roasted garlic, minced

1/2 cup canned low-salt chicken broth

1/2 cup cooked wild rice

2 cups cooked long grain brown rice

1 teaspoon dried thyme

1/3 cup sun-dried tomatoes

1 cup butternut squash, peeled, small dice

1/3 cup sunflower nuts, roasted and salted

1 cup sourdough bread crumbs

Melt butter in a large pot. Sauté onions and garlic until onions are translucent. Add broth and bring to a gentle boil. Add both rices and thyme. Add sun-dried tomatoes and squash. Cover and reduce heat. Cook until tender. Add sunflower nuts and bread crumbs. May be stuffed into your favorite bird or baked in the oven.

Yield: about 4 1/2 cups dressing

Sunday June 16th 1805.

she complains principally of the lower region of the abdomen, I therefore continued the cataplasms of barks and laudnumn which had been previously used by my friend Capt Clark. I beleive her disorder originated principally from an obstruction of the mensis in consequence of taking could.--

Meriwether Lewis

Squash and Buffalo Bake

1 pound ground buffalo (substitute beef)

2 Tablespoons canola oil

1/2 teaspoon kosher salt

fresh ground black pepper to taste

1 medium butternut squash, peeled, seeded and cubed

1 medium carrot, peeled and sliced

1 small yellow onion, diced

1/2 green bell pepper, large dice

1 cup cooked wild rice

1 cup cooked white rice

1/4 cup dried blueberries

1/4 cup salted and roasted sunflower nuts

3/4 teaspoon each of these dried herbs: thyme, tarragon, basil and sage

2 chipotle peppers, diced

4 cloves garlic, minced

Sauce:

1 cup sour cream

1/4 cup heavy cream

4-5 sun-dried tomatoes, cut into matchsticks

grated Parmesan cheese

Preheat oven to 350 degrees F. Brown buffalo meat in oil, with salt and pepper over low heat. In a large bowl, combine squash, carrot, onion, bell pepper, rices, blueberries, sunflower nuts, spices, chipotle pepper and garlic. Combine sauce ingredients, except for Parmesan cheese, in a separate small bowl. Add browned meat to vegetable and rice mixture. Pour sauce over mixture and transfer to an ovenproof casserole with a tight fitting lid and bake until squash is tender but still firm (about 50 minutes).

Garnish with Parmesan cheese. Serve with bread and salad.

Serves 4-6

Big Lake Duck and Wild Rice Salad

Marinade:

1/2 pound duck breast (substitute turkey) sliced into thin strips

1/4 cup extra virgin olive oil

1 Tablespoon honey

1 Tablespoon apple cider vinegar

1 Tablespoon hot and spicy prepared mustard

1 teaspoon kosher salt

1 medium yellow onion, diced

fresh ground black pepper to taste

Salad:

1 1/2 cups cooked wild rice

1 1/2 cups cooked brown rice

3 scallions, sliced thin

1/2 of a green bell pepper, small dice

5 ears pickled baby corn, sliced thin

1 medium carrot, small dice

1/3 cup sun-dried tomatoes, cut into thin strips

fresh ground black pepper to taste

Combine all marinade ingredients in a sealable plastic bag and marinate in the refrigerator for 60 minutes, turning at least once. Place entire contents of marinade bag in a heavy skillet over medium low heat. In a large mixing bowl, combine salad ingredients. When the meat is well browned, add entire contents of skillet to salad mixture and toss well. Allow flavors to blend at least 10 minutes.

This salad may also be served chilled, in a bowl lined with dark green leaf lettuce.

Serves 3-5

Buffalo Strip Salad

Marinade:

3/4 pound buffalo, cut into small strips or cubes

1/3 cup canola oil

1-2 Tablespoons soy sauce

juice from 1/2 lime

1 clove roasted garlic, minced

1/4 teaspoon hot pepper sauce

fresh ground black pepper to taste

Salad:

6 dark green lettuce leaves, torn into small pieces

1 ripe tomato cut into 8 wedges

1 medium carrot, large grate

1 cup of small cauliflower florets

1/2 cup cucumber, peeled, seeded and diced

1/4 cup each of chopped pecans, roasted and salted sunflower nuts and raisins (or currants)

2 scallions, sliced thin

Dressing:

2/3 cup safflower oil

3 Tablespoons black raspberry vinegar

2 Tablespoons chokecherry syrup

1 teaspoon kosher salt

juice from 1/2 lime

lots of fresh ground black pepper

Place all marinade ingredients in a large sealable plastic bag, shake and marinate in refrigerator for at least 40 minutes, turning once. Empty contents of bag into a large heavy skillet over medium low heat and brown until just done. Place contents of skillet into a colander and allow excess liquid to drain off. Place salad ingredients in a large serving bowl and top with well-drained meat. Whisk dressing ingredients together, pour over salad and toss lightly.

Serve with sourdough toast.

Serves 5-7 as a side salad

Great Northern Bean and Pecan Salad

Salad:
1 16-ounce can great northern beans, drained

1 1/4 cups cooked rice

3/4 cup pecans, chopped

1 medium tomato, seeded and diced

1/4 cup shredded carrot

1 medium cucumber, seeded, peeled and diced

3 scallions, sliced thin

2 teaspoons fresh jalapeno pepper, seeded and diced

12 fresh basil leaves, minced

Dressing:
1/2 cup extra virgin olive oil

2 Tablespoons balsamic vinegar

2 Tablespoons water

2 cloves roasted garlic, minced

1/2-1 teaspoon kosher salt

fresh ground black pepper to taste

Place all salad ingredients in a large bowl. Whisk all dressing ingredients together in a small bowl. Drizzle dressing over salad and toss lightly. May be served slightly chilled.

Serves 4-6

Tuesday 18th June 1805.

our Intrepters wife Some what better than She has been for Some time past. we are now 2580 1/4 miles from the mouth of the Missourie River.--

John Ordway

Nancy's Chicken and Cucumber Salad

1 1/2 pounds roasted chicken breast, diced

1 large cucumber peeled, seeded and diced

3 scallions, sliced thin

3-4 ounces pineapple juice

1 Tablespoon each of: lemon juice, soy sauce, olive oil, Worcestershire sauce

1/2 teaspoon hot pepper sauce

1/2 teaspoon fresh ginger, minced

Place chicken, cucumber and scallions in a bowl. Combine remaining ingredients together in another bowl, pour over chicken mixture and toss lightly. Allow flavors to blend at least 30 minutes.

May be served chilled.

Serves 2-3

Monday June 17th 1805.

The Indian woman much better today, I have still continued the same course of medecine; she is free from pain clear of fever, her pulse regular, and eats as heartily as I am willing to permit her of broiled buffaloe well seasoned with pepper and salt and rich soope of the same meat; I think therefore that there is every rational hope of her recovery.

Meriwether Lewis

Smoked Turkey and Wild Rice Salad

3/4 pound smoked, cooked turkey breast, large dice

1 cup cooked wild rice

1 cup cooked brown rice

1 cup cooked red beans, drained

1 Tablespoon olive oil

1/4 cup diced red bell pepper

1/4 cup diced green bell pepper

1/4 cup diced carrots

1/4 cup diced celery

1/2 cup diced mushrooms

1/2 teaspoon kosher salt

1/4 cup dried blueberries

1/4 salted and roasted sunflower nuts

3/4 cup extra virgin olive oil

2 Tablespoons prepared mustard

2 Tablespoons cider vinegar

2 Tablespoons water

2 teaspoons dark honey

1 teaspoon kosher salt

1 clove roasted garlic, minced

fresh ground black pepper to taste

several leaves of dark green lettuce

smoked Gouda (or other hard cheese)

1 small tomato, diced

fresh basil, chopped

Place meat, rices and beans in a medium bowl. In a skillet over medium low heat, place the oil, bell peppers, carrots, celery and mushrooms. Toss until coated and add 1/2 teaspoon kosher salt. Sauté for several minutes, then add to bowl. Add blueberries and sunflower nuts to bowl. Whisk or blend remaining ingredients together, add to bowl and toss until well coated. Allow flavors to blend at least 20 minutes. Line a serving bowl with lettuce leaves and place salad inside lined bowl.

May be served slightly chilled. Garnish individual servings with a little diced, smoked Gouda or other hard cheese, diced tomato and a little chopped fresh basil.

Serves 4-6

Buffalo Barley Salad

Marinade:
3/4 pound buffalo roast or steak, cut into
    1/4 by 1-inch strips (substitute beef)
1/4 cup canola oil
1/4 cup apple cider vinegar
1/4 cup red onion, diced
1/4 cup green bell pepper, diced
1/4 cup red bell pepper, diced
1/4 teaspoon dried thyme
1/4 teaspoon kosher salt
fresh ground black pepper to taste

Salad:
1 1/3 cups cooked barley
1/3 cup cooked wild rice
1/4 cup carrot, diced
1/4 cup celery, diced
1/2 cup small broccoli florets
1/4 cup red bell pepper, diced
1/4 cup red onion, diced

Dressing:
1/2 cup sesame tahini
1/2 cup extra virgin olive oil
the juice from one large lemon
    (about 1/4 cup)
1/4 cup soy sauce
1 clove garlic, minced
tomato wedges
toasted sesame seeds

Combine all marinade ingredients in a sealable plastic bag and marinate in the refrigerator for at least 60 minutes. Place all salad ingredients in a large bowl. In a medium mixing bowl, whisk the tahini and oil together until smooth and creamy. Gradually add in the soy sauce. Add the lemon juice a little at a time and whisk thoroughly. Add garlic if desired. Pour contents of plastic marinade bag, including all liquid, into a heavy skillet over low heat. When the meat is just done, remove from heat and drain in a colander to remove excess liquid. Add meat to salad and toss lightly. Add as much dressing as needed to flavor salad, or as much as you like.

Garnish with tomato wedges and toasted sesame seeds.

Serve with your favorite flat bread for lunch.

Serves 4-6

Grain and Buffalo Bake

1 pound ground buffalo (substitute beef)

2 Tablespoons canola oil

1/2 teaspoon kosher salt

fresh ground black pepper to taste

1 medium butternut squash, peeled, seeded and cubed

1 medium carrot, peeled and sliced

1 small yellow onion, diced

1/2 green bell pepper, large dice

1 cup cooked wild rice

1 cup cooked white rice

1/4 cup dried blueberries

1/4 cup salted and roasted sunflower nuts

3/4 teaspoon each of these dried herbs: thyme, tarragon, basil and sage

2 chipotle peppers, diced

4 cloves garlic, minced

1 cup sour cream

1/4 cup heavy cream

4-5 sun-dried tomatoes, cut into matchsticks

grated Parmesan cheese

Brown the buffalo with oil, salt and pepper over low heat. In a large bowl, combine squash, carrot, onion, bell pepper, rices, blueberries, sunflower nuts and spices. Combine remaining ingredients, except for Parmesan cheese, in a separate small bowl. Add browned meat to vegetable and rice mixture. Pour sauce over mixture and transfer to an ovenproof casserole with a tight fitting lid and bake until squash is tender but still firm (about 50 minutes).

Garnish with a little Parmesan cheese.

Serve with bread and salad.

Serves 4-6

Judith River Wild Rice Salad

Salad:
2 cups cooked wild rice

2 cups cooked white rice

1/2 cup celery, thinly sliced

1/2 cup fennel stalk, thinly sliced

1/2 cup sweet red pepper, diced

1/2 cup sweet peas, blanched

1/2 cup dried raspberries

1/2 cup onion, diced

1/2 cup hazelnuts, chopped

1-2 sprigs fresh basil, minced

Dressing:
1/3 cup chokecherry syrup

1/2 cup apple cider vinegar

1 Tablespoon extra virgin olive oil

3/4 teaspoon salt

fresh ground black pepper to taste

Place all salad ingredients in a large bowl. Whisk all dressing ingredients together in a small bowl.

Drizzle dressing over salad immediately before serving and toss lightly.

Serves 6

¹ Judith River, meeting the Missouri in Fergus County, Montana, still bears the name Clark gave it, after Julia (or Judith) Hancock, of Fincastle, Virginia, whom he married in 1808.

Thursday August 8th 1805

the Indian woman recognized the point of a
high plain to our right which she informed us
was not very distant from the summer retreat
of her nation on a river beyond the mountains
which runs to the west. this hill says her nation
calls the beaver's head from a conceived
remblance of it's figure to the head of that
animal. she assures us that we shall either find
her people on this river or on the river
immediately west of it's source; which from it's
present size cannot be very distant. as it is
now all important with us to meet with those
people as soon as possible...

Meriwether Lewis

"Western Landscape"
John Mix Stanley c.1847/1849, Gift of Dexter M. Ferry, Jr.
Photograph© 1984, The Detroit Institute of Arts

"Lewis and Clark Expedition"

Charles M. Russell (1846-1926), American — 1918, Oil on canvas, 30 1/2" X 48 1/2"

From the collection of Gilcrease Museum, Tulsa, Oklahoma

From the Garden

Saturday August 17th 1805.
Shortly after Capt. Clark arrived with the Interpreter Charbono, and the Indian woman, who proved to be a sister of the Chif Cameahwait. the meeting of those people was really affecting, particularly between Sah cah-gar-we-ah and an Indian woman, who had been taken prisoner at the same time with her, and who had afterwards escaped from the Minnetares and rejoined her nation.

Meriwether Lewis

Mandan Stew

1 pound buffalo, cubed (substitute elk, venison or beef)

1/2 medium onion, chopped

4 cups water

1 1/2 teaspoons hickory smoked salt

2 medium potatoes, peeled and cubed

1 medium butternut squash, cubed

2 bay leaves

1/2 cup sweet corn, cut off the cob

1 teaspoon dried crushed sage

1 teaspoon ground mace

1 teaspoon dried sweet basil leaves

1 cup shredded cabbage

3/4 cup shredded jerky (smoked)

Preheat oven to 325 degrees F. Place buffalo and onion in ovenproof 2-quart saucepan. Cover and place in a preheated oven for 1 hour. Buffalo should be brown and tender. Remove from oven and place on stove. Add water, salt, potatoes, squash and bay leaves. Simmer covered for 30 minutes or until potatoes are cooked. Add corn, the rest of the spices, cabbage and jerky. Simmer uncovered for an additional 20 minutes.

Garnish with salted sunflower seeds.

Serves 3-5

Saturday August 17th 1805

We halted our Canoes, when a number of the Snake Nation of Indians came to us; these were the Persons who we had heard singing; They informed us by our Interpreter (the Indian Woman) that Captain Lewis & party was at the Forks of the River waiting for us.--

Joseph Whitehouse

Garden Stir Fry

Marinade:

3/4 pound venison, cut into thin strips
   (substitute buffalo, elk or beef)

3 Tablespoons canola oil or olive oil

1 Tablespoon soy sauce

1 Tablespoon honey

1 Tablespoon lemon juice

2 cloves garlic, minced

1 teaspoon hot pepper sauce

Stir Fry:

1/2 cup squash, peeled and diced and
   steamed until just done

1 medium onion, diced

1/2 cup roasted sunflower nuts

1 potato peeled, diced and steamed
   until just done

1 1/2 cups mushrooms, diced

2 ribs celery cut thin on the diagonal

Combine marinade ingredients in a sealable bag and refrigerate for at least 1 hour.
In a large skillet, sauté marinade mixture over medium high heat until meat is
nearly done. Reduce heat and add the remaining ingredients and stir fry until
celery is tender crisp.

Serve with wild rice.

Serves 3-5

Friday August 16th 1805

I had mentioned to the chief several times that we had with us a woman of
his nation who had been taken prisoner by the Minnetares, and that by
means of her I hoped to explain myself more fully than I could do by signs.

Meriwether Lewis

Squash Curry

2 medium white onions, large dice

2 Tablespoons extra virgin olive oil

2 Tablespoons butter

1 teaspoon kosher salt

2 Tablespoons curry powder

3 cups winter squash, peeled, seeded and cubed

4 scallions, sliced

2 Tablespoons red bell pepper, minced

1/2 cup roasted and salted sunflower nuts

1/2 teaspoon hot pepper sauce (optional)

2 cups cooked kidney beans, drained

water as needed

Place onions, olive oil and butter in a large heavy skillet over medium to medium low heat. Stir to coat onions and add salt. Sauté, stirring occasionally, until onions are tender yet firm. Add curry powder and stir until onions are coated. Add remaining ingredients, except for kidney beans and stir to coat with onion/curry mixture. Reduce heat and simmer, stirring frequently, until squash is tender yet firm. Add kidney beans and cook several minutes more. Add water during cooking as needed to keep the mixture from sticking to bottom of pan. Remove from heat and allow flavors to blend 5 minutes.

Garnish with a few sliced scallions and a little plain yogurt, if desired. Serve as a side dish with venison or elk.

Serves 3-4

Green Cabbage & Red Onions With Buffalo Sausage

Sausage:

NOTE: The sausage needs to be prepared at least 2 hours ahead of time.

1 pound ground buffalo (substitute beef or elk)

1 Tablespoon canola oil

1 Tablespoon brown sugar, firmly packed

2 cloves garlic, minced

1 Tablespoon white sesame seeds

1 teaspoon kosher salt

1 teaspoon dried basil

1 teaspoon sweet Hungarian paprika

1/2 teaspoon hot pepper sauce

fresh ground black pepper to taste

Combine all ingredients in a bowl. Mix well, cover bowl with food wrap and place in refrigerator for at least 2 hours or overnight.

Vegetable Mixture:

2 Tablespoons canola oil

6 cups green cabbage, diced

1 red onion, sliced in rings

1 teaspoon kosher salt

fresh ground black pepper to taste

1 15-ounce can black beans, drained

juice from one lime

10-12 fresh basil leaves, chopped

Place sausage and canola oil in a large Dutch oven over medium low heat. When sausage begins to brown, add cabbage, onions, salt and pepper; stirring occasionally. When cabbage has begun to soften, add beans. When cabbage is tender yet firm, remove Dutch oven from heat and add lime juice. Chop fresh basil and add to Dutch oven. Stir quickly and serve immediately with rice or potatoes.

Serves 6

Missouri Garden Mash

6 medium potatoes, boiled and peeled

3-4 cups green cabbage, diced and
    steamed

1 small red onion, small dice

2 teaspoons kosher salt

3 Tablespoons butter

coarsely ground fresh black pepper to
    taste

Place warm potatoes and cabbage in a Dutch oven and mash. Add remaining
ingredients and mash. Cover and allow flavors to blend 5 minutes.

Serve warm with a little butter on each serving and a dash of paprika. Serve with
poultry or meat (pork, venison or buffalo).

Serves 4-6

August 17th Satturday 1805
The Great Chief of this nation proved to be the brother of the
Woman with us and is a man of Influence Sence & easey & reserved
manners, appears to possess a great deel of Cincerity.

William Clark

Curried Zucchini Salad

3 small, fresh zucchini, peeled and
  diced

3 scallions, sliced thin

1/2 cup plain yogurt

1/2 cup mayonnaise

2 Tablespoons butter

2 Tablespoons curry powder

fresh ground black pepper to taste

Place zucchini and scallions in a bowl. In a separate bowl, combine yogurt and mayonnaise. Melt butter in a small skillet over medium low heat. Add curry powder and pepper stirring continuously until mixture has darkened and curry powder is cooked. Add to yogurt/mayonnaise mixture and stir well. Add to vegetables, stir until vegetables are well-coated and allow flavors to blend 10-15 minutes.

May be served chilled. Serve with your favorite entrée.

Yield: about 2 1/2 cups

Green Beans With Bacon and Onion

3-4 strips bacon
1/2 pound fresh green beans, steamed and cut in 2-inch diagonals
1/2 cup white onion, small dice
fresh ground black pepper to taste
toasted sesame seeds

Fry bacon, remove from pan; drain and crumble. Add green beans and onion to skillet and sauté lightly in bacon drippings. When onions are tender, add crumbled bacon back to skillet and add pepper as desired.

Garnish with toasted sesame seeds if desired.

Serve as a side with your favorite entrée or as a topping on potatoes, rice or pasta.

Serves 2-3

Wednesday August 14th
this evening Charbono struck his indian Woman for which Capt. C. gave him a severe repremand.

Meriwether Lewis

Roasted Tomato Salsa

1 pound ripe red tomatoes, roasted (blackened) and chopped (with skins)
1/2 cup onion, chopped
juice from 1 lime
2 cloves roasted garlic, minced
1 teaspoon kosher salt
1 jalapeno pepper, minced
1 Tablespoon cilantro, minced
1/4 teaspoon honey
fresh ground black pepper to taste

Combine ingredients in a bowl. Chill.

Serve with chips.

Yield: about 2 cups

August 14th Wednesday 1805
I checked our interpreter for Strikeing his woman at their Dinner.

William Clark

89

Three Rivers Vegetable Lasagna

Vegetables:
1 Tablespoon olive oil

1/2 cup chopped onion

1/2 cups frozen sweet corn kernels

1 cup peeled, grated carrots

2 cups small zucchini, peeled and chopped

3 large mushrooms, chopped

1 turnip, small dice

Sauce Mixture:
2 14 1/2-ounce cans whole peeled tomatoes, chopped

1 6-ounce can tomato paste

1 cup water

1 teaspoon brown sugar, firmly packed

pinch of anise seed

1/2 teaspoon fresh ground black pepper

1 Tablespoon finely chopped fresh basil leaves

1/2 teaspoon hickory smoked salt

1 bay leaf

1/2 teaspoon liquid smoke

1/4 cup unsalted sunflower nuts

Cheese Mixture:
1 cup Parmesan cheese, grated

2 cups Ricotta cheese

1/4 cup chopped cilantro

2 Tablespoons sweet basil, chopped

1 10-ounce package frozen spinach, thawed and drained

1 pound Mozzarella cheese, shredded

1 Tablespoon chopped pimientos

9 cooked and cooled lasagna noodles

(see next page)

Three Rivers Vegetable Lasagna (continued)

In a Dutch oven, sauté vegetables in olive oil over medium heat until onion is translucent. Add sauce ingredients and simmer for 15 minutes. Preheat oven to 350 degrees F. In an 8 1/2x11-inch cake pan, make the following layers.

1. half of the sauce mixture
2. three noodles
3. half of the cheese mixture
4. one-third of the mozzarella cheese
5. three noodles
6. the other half of the cheese mixture
7. one-third of the mozzarella cheese
8. three noodles
9. the rest of the sauce mixture
10. one-third of the mozzarella cheese

Cover with tin foil and bake for 30 minutes or until cheese is melted.

Yield: 5-7 servings

Beans and Eggs Sacagawea

2 Tablespoons butter

1/2 cup onion, chopped

2 Tablespoons sun-dried tomatoes in oil, chopped

1 teaspoon garlic, minced

1/4 cup corn

1 can (4 1/2-ounce) chopped green chilies

1 15-ounce can black beans, drained

2 teaspoons chili powder

1 cup cooked rice

6 eggs, beaten

2 Tablespoons butter

4 ounces cream cheese

1 cup Havarti with Jalapeno cheese, shredded

chili powder as garnish

salted and roasted sunflower nuts

sour cream

Sauté onions, tomatoes, garlic and corn in a large skillet over medium heat with butter until onions are translucent. Add chilies, beans, rice and chili powder and stir. Remove from heat. In another skillet over medium heat, cook the eggs in butter, flipping once. Reduce heat to low and add chunks of cream cheese on eggs, then add the onion mixture. Top with Havarti and cover until cheese has melted. Sprinkle with a little more chili powder.

Garnish with salted and roasted sunflower nuts and sour cream.

Serves 3-5

Groundnut Pumpkin Sauce

1 medium onion, chopped

2 cloves garlic, minced

1 Tablespoon butter

1 cup chicken broth

1 cup cooked pumpkin, purée

3/4 cup crunchy peanut butter

1/2-1 teaspoon ground red pepper

1 Tablespoon oyster sauce

1/4 teaspoon ground ginger

In a large skillet, sauté onion and garlic until onion is translucent. Add the rest of the ingredients and simmer for 15 minutes stirring frequently.

Serve with meat.

Yield: About 3 cups

August 15th Thursday 1805

In walking on Shore I Saw Several rattle Snakes and narrowly escaped at two different times, as also the Squar when walking with her husband on Shore-- I killed a Buck nothing else killed to day-- This mountn. I call rattle Snake mountain.

William Clark

Mushroom Bake

Mushroom Mixture:

2 cups mushrooms, chopped

1/4 cup onions, chopped

1 Tablespoon scallions, minced

1 Tablespoon sun-dried tomatoes in oil, chopped

1 teaspoon minced garlic

1 Tablespoon butter

1 Tablespoon canola oil

1 Tablespoon whole wheat flour

1/4 cup cold milk

1/4 teaspoon salt

Egg Mixture:

1/2 cup whole wheat flour

2 cups cold milk

3 Tablespoons butter

1/2 teaspoon salt

fresh ground pepper to taste

1/8 teaspoon ground nutmeg

4 eggs, at room temperature

1 1/2 cups grated Cheddar cheese

Preheat oven to 400 degrees F. Sauté mushrooms, onions, tomatoes and garlic in butter and oil. When onions are translucent, sprinkle flour over mixture. Stir in milk and continue to stir until mixture is thick. Stir in salt, remove from heat and set aside. In a medium sauce pan, whisk milk into flour. Place over medium heat, stirring constantly. When mixture is thick and bubbly, remove from heat and stir in the butter and seasonings. Stir in the eggs, one at a time. Add 1 cup of the shredded cheese. Butter a medium casserole dish. Pour 1/2 of the egg mixture in the casserole. Next, spoon the mushroom mixture on top of the egg mixture. Top with the remaining egg mixture. Sprinkle with the remaining cheese. Place in preheated oven and bake uncovered for 25 minutes.

Serve immediately.

Serves 6

Meriwether's Sweet Potatoes

1 large sweet potato, peeled and cut in 1/2 inch thick half rounds, steamed

2 large eggs

1/2 teaspoon vanilla extract

2 Tablespoons sifted all-purpose white flour

3 Tablespoons minced pecans

2 Tablespoons maple sugar *(substitute: 2 Tablespoons brown sugar)*

1/8 teaspoon kosher salt

1/2 teaspoon ground cinnamon

1/4 teaspoon ground nutmeg

dash of fresh ground black pepper

maple syrup

1 pint peanut oil

In a medium bowl, whisk eggs with vanilla extract. In a separate bowl add flour, pecans, maple sugar, salt, cinnamon, nutmeg, and pepper. Mix thoroughly. Heat oil. Dip potatoes into egg wash and then into dry ingredients. Carefully add to hot oil. Brown on both sides and remove. Drizzle with maple syrup. Serve hot.

Serves 3

Baked Beans

1 pound great northern or navy beans,
    soaked in water overnight

3 ounces tomato paste

3/4 cup maple syrup

1/4 cup molasses

2 Tablespoons prepared horseradish
    mustard

2 Tablespoons soy sauce or 1/2 pound
    smoked ham, diced

1 small onion, diced

1 carrot, sliced thin

2 cloves garlic, minced

1 whole dried bay leaf

1 Tablespoon canola or olive oil

boiling water to cover 1 inch above
    beans

Preheat oven to 225 degrees F. Drain soaking water off of beans. Place all ingredients in a large Dutch oven. Bring to a boil over medium heat, stirring frequently. Reduce heat to low and cook beans for 10-15 minutes, stirring frequently. Place lid on Dutch oven, transfer to oven and bake for approximately 4 hours or until beans are soft. Check liquid level at 2 1/2 hours; adding more boiling water if beans are too dry. Remove pot from oven, discard bay leaf and stir thoroughly. Replace lid and allow flavors to blend for 60 minutes before serving.

Serve as a side dish with meat or poultry.

Serves 6-9

Garden Corn Bake

10 ounces frozen whole kernel corn

1/4 cup onion, chopped

1/4 cup red bell pepper, minced

2 Tablespoons butter

2 Tablespoons all-purpose white flour

1 teaspoon kosher salt

1/2 teaspoon paprika

1/4 teaspoon dry mustard

dash fresh ground black pepper

3/4 cup whole milk

1/2 cup cheddar cheese, shredded

1 egg, slightly beaten

1/3 cup dried sourdough bread, crumbled

1/4 cup sunflower nuts, salted and roasted

1 Tablespoon butter, melted

Heat oven to 350 degrees F. Sauté onion and red pepper in 2 Tablespoons butter until onion is translucent. Remove from heat. Stir in flour and seasonings. Cook over low heat. Gradually stir in milk. Heat to boiling, stirring constantly. Boil and stir 1 minute. Stir in corn, cheese and egg. Pour into ungreased 1-quart casserole. Combine sourdough crumbs, sunflower nuts, and 1 Tablespoon melted butter; sprinkle evenly over corn mixture. Bake uncovered 30-35 minutes.

Serve as a side dish.

Serves 4-6

Thursday August 15th 1805.

Capt Clark was very near being bitten twice today by rattlesnakes, the Indian woman also narrowly escaped.

Meriwether Lewis

Thursday [NB: Saturday} 21st Septr. 1805

The Cheif drew me a kind of chart of the
river, and informed me a greater Cheif than
himself was fishing at the river half a days
march from his village called the twisted hare,
and that the river forked a little below his
Camp⁹ and at a long distance below & below 2
large forks one from he left & the other from
the right¹⁰ the river passed thro'gh the
mountains at which place was a great fall of
the water passing through the rocks,

William Clark

"Shoshone Falls on the Snake River"

Thomas Moran (1837-1926), American, born England — 1900, Oil on canvas, 71" X 132"

From the collection of Gilcrease Museum, Tulsa, Oklahoma

"Angry River"
John F. Clymer — 1978, Oil
Courtesy of Clymer Museum & Gallery, Ellensburg, Washington

Big Game

October 21st Monday 1805

imediately above & below this little river comences a rapid which is crouded with large rocks in every direction, the pasage both crooked and dificuelt, we halted at a Lodge to examine thos noumerous Islands of rock which apd. to extend maney miles below,-- .great numbs. of Indians came in Canoes to View us at this place, after passing this rapid which we accomplished without loss; <we passed> winding through between the hugh rocks for about 2 miles--.

William Clark

Drouillard's Elk Sauté

Marinade:

3/4 pound elk sirloin steak, cubed (substitute beef or venison)

2 cloves roasted garlic, minced

2 teaspoons fresh ginger, grated

1 teaspoon lemon zest

1/2 teaspoon hot pepper sauce

1 Tablespoon soy sauce

juice from 1 lemon

1 1/2 Tablespoons extra virgin olive oil

pinch of kosher salt

1/2 teaspoon fresh ground black pepper

Sauté:

1 1/2 cups squash, peeled, diced and steamed tender

1 medium onion, diced

1/2 cup roasted sunflower nuts

1 green pepper, large dice

1 1/2 cups mushrooms, diced

1 medium tomato, seeded and diced

Marinate meat in a sealable bag for at least 1 hour. Place marinade mixture in a large skillet over medium high heat and sauté until meat is done. Reduce heat and add the squash, onion, sun seeds, pepper and mushrooms. Cook, stirring occasionally until pepper is done. Toss with tomato and serve.

Serves 5

Wednesday 24th July, 1805

The morning was fine, and we early prosecuted our voyage; passed a bank of very red earth, which our squaw told us the natives use for paint. Deer are plenty among the bushes...

Patrick Gass

Hell's Gate Elk Strip Steak

Marinade:

1 pound elk round steak, cut into strips
   (substitute buffalo or beef)

2 Tablespoons extra virgin olive oil

2 Tablespoons apple cider vinegar

1/8 teaspoon liquid smoke

1 Tablespoon prepared yellow mustard

1/2 teaspoon hot pepper sauce

1 clove roasted garlic, minced

1 1/2 Tablespoons Worcestershire sauce

1/2 teaspoon kosher salt

Combine ingredients in a sealable bag. Marinate meat for at least 1 hour. Discard excess marinade. Grill until just done.

Serve with *Melon Salsa* (see recipe page 174) and corn bread.

Serves 2-3

103

Stovetop Venison Steaks in Barbecue Sauce

1 1/2-2 pounds venison steaks (substitute beef, elk or buffalo)

1 cup tomato sauce

3 Tablespoons chopped scallions

1 Tablespoon tomato paste

1/4 cup canola oil

1/3 cup molasses

3 Tablespoons honey

1/4 cup (scant) apple cider vinegar

2 cloves garlic, minced

1 teaspoon kosher salt

1 teaspoon dried ground thyme

1/2 teaspoon hot pepper sauce

fresh ground black pepper to taste

Place steaks in a large, sealable plastic bag. Combine remaining ingredients in a blender and purèe until smooth. Add to bag with steaks, seal and marinate in refrigerator for at least 90 minutes, turning at least once. Empty contents of bag into a large heavy skillet with a tight fitting lid. Bring to a low boil, cover, reduce heat and simmer until meat is tender. Remove lid and allow flavors to blend 15 minutes.

Serve with wild rice and a green salad.

Serves 3-4

Juniper Buffalo Stick Roast

1 pound buffalo round steak, sliced 1/2 inch thick and 5-6 inches long (substitute elk or beef)

1 Tablespoon juniper berries, crushed

1/4 cup canola oil

1/4 cup rice vinegar

3/4 teaspoon hickory smoked salt

1/2 teaspoon fresh ground black pepper

2 Tablespoons onion, minced

1/4 teaspoon ground cayenne pepper

1/8 teaspoon liquid smoke

2 teaspoons Worcestershire sauce

1 cup beef broth

scallions, chopped

Place all ingredients except for beef broth in a large sealable plastic bag. Make sure all meat is coated. Place bag in shallow pan. Marinate overnight in refrigerator, turning bag at least once. Skewer the meat lengthwise. Pour excess marinade into a small saucepan. Add beef broth to marinade and bring to a boil. Reduce heat and simmer for 20 minutes or until liquid is reduced by half. Grill skewers over hot coals to preference. (Remember buffalo cooks about twice as fast as beef, so reduce grill heat). Place meat on platter and pour cooked marinade over meat.

Garnish with chopped scallions.

Serves 3-5

Clark's Pan-fried Venison With Mustard Sauce

3 Tablespoons sifted all-purpose white flour

1/2 teaspoon salt

fresh ground black pepper to taste

4 venison sirloin steaks, or pounded venison round steaks (substitute beef, elk or buffalo)

2 Tablespoons olive oil

1/2 cup chicken broth

2 teaspoons coarse ground prepared mustard

1 teaspoon ground horseradish

2 Tablespoons cream cheese

sunflower nuts

Combine flour, salt and pepper in a shallow dish and dredge the meat in the seasoned flour. Place the oil in a large skillet over medium high heat. Add the meat and brown both sides. Turn heat to low and simmer until the meat is done. In a medium saucepan, combine broth, mustard, horseradish and cream cheese over medium heat. Do not boil. When ready to serve, pour sauce over meat.

Garnish with sunflower nuts.

Serves 4

Buffalo on a Stick

1 pound buffalo sirloin cut into strips (substitute venison, elk or beef)

1/3 cup canola oil

1 Tablespoon apple cider vinegar

1 teaspoon kosher salt

1/2 teaspoon liquid smoke

1/2 teaspoon fresh ground black pepper

Combine all ingredients in a sealable plastic bag. Marinate for 2-3 hours or in the refrigerator overnight. Discard excess marinade. Skewer and grill meat according to preference and serve.

Great with a salad or in a taco.

Serves 3-4

107

Buffalo Hash

canola oil

kosher salt

fresh ground black pepper to taste

3/4 pound cooked buffalo meat, in small cubes (substitute beef or elk)

3 small potatoes, peeled and cubed

1 large carrot cut in 1/4 inch rounds

1/2 cup green bell pepper, diced

1/2 cup red bell pepper, diced

1 small onion, large dice

1 cup corn kernels

1/2 cup salted and roasted sunflower nuts

1/4 cup ketchup

1/4 cup coarse ground prepared mustard

Combine all ingredients in a large skillet over medium low heat stirring frequently. When potatoes are just done, remove from heat and allow flavors to blend for 5 minutes.

Serve with fresh bread and pickles.

Yield: 4 cups

Marinated Venison Steaks With Sesame Squash Sauce

Marinade:
1 1/2 pounds venison steaks cut into thin strips (substitute beef, elk or buffalo)
1/2 cup canola oil
1/4 cup cider vinegar
2 cloves roasted garlic, minced
1 teaspoon kosher salt
lots of fresh ground black pepper

Sauce:
1/4 cup onion, very small dice
1 Tablespoon canola oil
1 cup cooked butternut squash
1/4 cup sesame tahini
2 Tablespoons soy sauce
chopped fresh scallions or chives

Combine all marinade ingredients in a sealable plastic bag and marinate in the refrigerator for at least 2 hours, turning at least once.

Combine all sauce ingredients in a blender or food processor, purée until smooth. Remove meat from marinade and grill or broil until just done but not dried out. Discard excess marinade. Transfer sauce from blender into saucepan. Gently reheat on stove, do not boil. Discard excess marinade. Spoon a little sauce onto each plate, place steak on top of sauce and top with more sauce and scallions or chives as garnish.

Serve with sourdough bread and your favorite green salad.

Serves 3-4

Winter Venison Stew

1 1/2 pounds venison, cubed
   (substitute buffalo, elk or beef)

1 medium onion, large dice

2 Tablespoons canola oil or olive oil

2 whole dried bay leaves

1-2 teaspoons kosher salt

fresh ground black pepper to taste

2-3 cloves garlic, minced

3 medium carrots, peeled, cut in
   1-inch chunks

3 medium red potatoes, peeled and
   cubed

1 cup green cabbage, coarsely chopped

1 Tablespoon apple cider vinegar

1 Tablespoon brown sugar, firmly
   packed

1 cup chicken broth

1 15-ounce can stewed tomatoes,
   crushed, with liquid

1 15 1/2-ounce can great northern
   beans, with liquid

fresh chopped chives

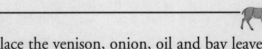

Place the venison, onion, oil and bay leaves in a large Dutch oven or soup pot over medium low heat. Stir until the mixture is well coated, then add salt and pepper. Brown mixture for several minutes, stirring constantly. Add remaining ingredients, bring to a boil and then reduce heat and simmer, uncovered, until venison is cooked all the way through and vegetables are tender.

Serve with **Sunny Corn Biscuits** (see recipe page 49) and a green salad.

Garnish with fresh chives.

Serves 3-5

Cath's Elk and Pepper Steak

1 pound elk sirloin, cut into strips (substitute buffalo or beef)

2 Tablespoons extra virgin olive oil

kosher salt to taste

1/2 teaspoon fresh ground black pepper

1 green bell pepper cut into strips

1 medium onion cut into 10 sections

4 large white mushrooms cut into strips

1 1/2 Tablespoons soy sauce

1 1/2 Tablespoons Worcestershire sauce

Place meat, oil, salt and pepper in a large skillet over medium low heat. When meat is browned, add remaining ingredients, stir, cover and reduce heat to simmer for an additional 30 minutes or until elk and vegetables are tender.

Serve over brown or wild rice with a tossed salad and fresh sourdough bread.

Serves 2-3

Venison with Potatoes and Sauerkraut

Marinade:

1 1/2 pounds venison, cut into strips
   (substitute buffalo, elk or beef)

1/3 cup extra virgin olive oil

2 Tablespoons red wine vinegar

1 Tablespoon granulated white sugar

1 Tablespoon soy sauce

1 Tablespoon Worcestershire sauce

1 teaspoon dark sesame oil

1 teaspoon hot pepper sauce

2 cloves garlic, quartered

lots of fresh ground black pepper

Vegetables:

1/2 pound baby carrots

3 medium red potatoes, peeled and cut
   into 6 pieces each

1 medium onion, cut into 8 wedges

1 14-ounce can sauerkraut, with liquid

Combine all marinade ingredients in a large sealable plastic bag and marinate in the refrigerator for at least 60 minutes, turning at least once. Place all ingredients in a large Dutch oven over medium low heat. When the mixture begins to boil, cover and reduce heat. Simmer for 60-70 minutes or until venison is cooked through and potatoes and carrots are tender.

Serves 3-5

French Canadian Buffalo Sausage

1/2 pound Canadian bacon

2 Tablespoons dried raspberries

1 pound ground buffalo (substitute beef)

2 Tablespoons safflower oil

1 Tablespoon lime juice

1 Tablespoon brown sugar, firmly packed

1 teaspoon fresh ground black pepper

1/4 teaspoon ground cayenne pepper

1/2 teaspoon hot pepper sauce

1/4 teaspoon ground nutmeg

1 teaspoon minced roasted garlic

1/2 teaspoon kosher salt

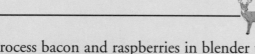

Process bacon and raspberries in blender until meat and berries are finely ground. Combine blended ingredients with the rest of ingredients. Cover and refrigerate overnight to allow flavors to mingle. Divide into 6 equal parts and form patties. Fry over medium low heat until done. (Do not over cook).

Yield: 6 patties

Sunday 18th, August 1805.

A fine morning, We bought three horses of the Indians. Captain Clarke and 11 more, with our interpreter and his wife, and all the Indians set out 11 o'clock to go over to the Columbia.--The Indians went for horses to carry our baggage, and we search for timber to make canoes for descending the Columbia.

Patrick Gass

Heart River Elk Kabobs

Marinade:

3/4 pound elk sirloin steak, cubed
   (substitute buffalo or beef)

2 Tablespoons canola oil

2 Tablespoons key lime juice

2 cloves roasted garlic, minced

1 Tablespoon brown sugar, firmly
   packed

2-3 teaspoons kosher salt

lots of fresh ground black pepper

Kabobs:

tomato wedges

green pepper

onion wedges

mushrooms

winter squash, peeled and steamed
   until tender but firm

Combine marinade ingredients in a sealable plastic bag. Marinate meat for at least 60 minutes. Skewer meat and vegetables. Brush skewers with marinade. Salt and pepper lightly. Grill until just done. Discard excess marinade.

Yield: 6 Skewers

Thursday August 22

Our Indian interpreter & his wife came over with those Indians, they were badly off for provisions, they had killed only 2 Mountain Sheep, or Ibex & some Rabits &ca.-- These Indians all encamped with us, & behave peacable, & do not attempt to steal any thing, & borrow nothing but what they return again.-- They appear to be in constant dread of the other Nations Indians, who are constantly at Warr with them.

Joseph Whitehouse

Prairie Buffalo Bake

Meat Mixture:

1 pound ground buffalo (substitute
beef or elk)

1 teaspoon salt

1/2 teaspoon ground poultry seasoning

1/2 teaspoon dried thyme leaves

1 Tablespoon onion, diced

Cheese Mixture:

8 ounces cream cheese, softened

1/4 cup onion, diced

1/2 cup mushrooms, diced

1/2 teaspoon minced garlic

2 Tablespoons sun-dried tomatoes in
oil, small dice

2 Tablespoons Parmesan cheese, grated

1/4 teaspoon salt

Topping:

1/2 cup shredded Mozzarella cheese

fresh ground black pepper to taste

Preheat oven to 325 degrees F. In two separate bowls, combine the ingredients for
the mixtures. Place half the meat mixture in a buttered loaf pan. Then, place the
cheese mixture over the meat, followed by the rest of the meat mixture. Cover pan
with aluminum foil and bake for 30 minutes. Remove from oven and top with
Mozzarella cheese and black pepper. Return to oven uncovered for 10 minutes or
until cheese is melted.

Serves 3-5

Saturday August 24th 1805.

I had now nine horses and a mule, and two which I had hired made twelve these I had loaded and the Indian women took the ballance of the baggage. I had given the Interpreter some articles with which to purchase a horse for the woman which he had obtained.

Meriwether Lewis

"A Sangeys Village on the Esquímalt"
Paul Kane (1810-1871) — 1847, Watercolor on paper, 5 1/4" X 8 7/8"
Courtesy of Stark Museum of Art, Orange, Texas

"Medicine Masks of the Northwest Coast Tribes"
Paul Kane (1810-1871) — 1847, Watercolor on paper, 5 1/2" X 8 3/4"
Courtesy of Stark Museum of Art, Orange, Texas

From the...
Sky

Tuesday Septemr. 10th 1805

The hunters went out again up the Creek a short distance, and came across 3 Indians on horse back, those Indians seemed afraid of our hunters, untill they laid down their Guns, they then came up to them in a friendly manner. these Indians took our hunters up behind them, and rode very fast down to our Camp, We learnt from our Interpreters & Guide, that those Indians belonged to a Nation of Indians called the Flatt head Nation.

Joseph Whitehouse

Grilled Chicken Breasts
With Chipotle Chocolate Sauce

4 chicken breasts, grilled or broiled

2 Tablespoons extra virgin olive oil

1 medium onion, small dice

2 cloves garlic, minced

2 whole chipotles in adobo sauce, minced

fresh ground black pepper to taste

kosher salt

1 teaspoon ground cinnamon

1/4 teaspoon ground coriander

1/4 teaspoon ground cloves

2 Tablespoons pecans, finely chopped

1 Tablespoon white sesame seeds

2 Tablespoons raisins, chopped

2 Tablespoons yellow cornmeal

2 teaspoons chopped fresh cilantro

1/2 cup tomato juice

2 cups chicken broth

1 ounce unsweetened baking chocolate, grated

1 Tablespoon black raspberry vinegar

1 Tablespoon honey

Place the olive oil and onion in a large heavy skillet over medium low heat. When onions have started to soften, add the garlic and chipotle peppers, stirring frequently. When onions are soft and translucent add the pepper, salt, cinnamon, coriander, cloves, pecans, sesame seeds, raisins, cornmeal and cilantro; stirring constantly. Add the tomato juice and broth, stirring constantly for several minutes. Reduce heat to simmer and allow mixture to reduce slightly, stirring occasionally. Add grated chocolate, stirring constantly until chocolate is completely melted. Add vinegar and honey and simmer for 5 minutes, stirring frequently. If a smoother texture is desired, the sauce may be cooled slightly and puréed. Spoon sauce over chicken breast and garnish with a little fresh cilantro or chopped scallions.

Serve with corn bread and a green salad.

Serves 4

BBQ Chicken With Garden Sauté

Marinade:

1 pound chicken breasts, cut into thin
    1-inch strips or cubed

1 cup barbecue sauce

juice from 1/2 lime

fresh ground black pepper to taste

Sauté:

1/2 pound fresh green beans, cut into
    2-inch pieces

10 baby carrots, each cut into 4 pieces

1/2 cup roasted & salted sunflower nuts

3 Tablespoons diced dried Bing cherries

2 Tablespoons extra virgin olive oil

fresh ground black pepper to taste

1/2 teaspoon hot pepper sauce

1/2 cup finely diced yellow bell pepper

1/2 cup finely diced red onion

juice from 1/2 lime

6-8 fresh basil leaves, chopped

Combine all marinade ingredients in a sealable plastic bag and marinate in refrigerator for at least one hour. In a large heavy skillet, over medium heat, empty contents of marinade bag. Stir constantly for 1-2 minutes and add remaining ingredients, except for fresh basil. Sauté, stirring frequently. When chicken and green beans are done, remove from heat and add fresh basil.

Toss lightly and serve immediately with rice or potatoes.

Serves 3-4

Marinated Chicken and Garden Kabobs

Marinade:
2/3 cup extra virgin olive oil

6 Tablespoons white balsamic vinegar

2 teaspoons Italian seasoning

2 teaspoons salt

Meat:
2 large chicken breasts, cut into 1-inch cubes

Vegetables:
1/2 large red onion, chunked

2 small zucchinis, peeled, chunked and steamed

1 butternut squash, peeled, chunked and steamed

1/4 small head of cabbage, chunked

2 medium tomatoes, cut in chunks

If using wooden skewers, soak overnight in water or skewers will burn up on grill. In a large sealable plastic bag, combine half of marinade with vegetables. Allow to marinate for several hours. In another sealable plastic bag, combine remaining marinade with the cubed chicken. Allow to marinate in the refrigerator for several hours. Alternate vegetables with chicken on skewers. Discard marinade.

Grill over hot coals until chicken is done. (About 8 minutes, each side).

Serves 3-4

Saturday 14th Sept. 1805

our <Intrepter>Guide tells us that the natives catch a great nomber of Sammon along here. we went down the creek abt. 4 miles and Camped for the night. Eat a little portable Soup, but the men in jeneral So hungry that we killed a fine Colt which eat verry well, at this time.

Joseph Whitehouse

Smoked Turkey and Portabella Lasagna

8-10 lasagna noodles, cooked and chilled

1 1/2 cups heavy cream

2 cups cottage cheese

1/2 cup sour cream

4 Tablespoons all-purpose white flour

1/2 teaspoon each of dried basil, oregano, thyme and black pepper

1 medium white onion, chopped

1 red bell pepper, diced

1-2 large portabella mushrooms, sliced thin

1 pound smoked turkey breast, julienne-cut

14 ounces smoked Gouda cheese, shredded

1 6-ounce can black olives, drained and sliced

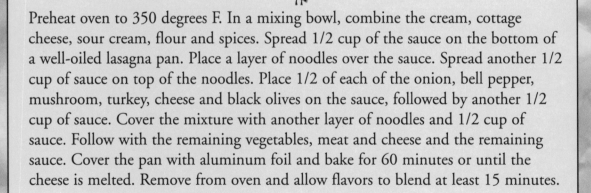

Preheat oven to 350 degrees F. In a mixing bowl, combine the cream, cottage cheese, sour cream, flour and spices. Spread 1/2 cup of the sauce on the bottom of a well-oiled lasagna pan. Place a layer of noodles over the sauce. Spread another 1/2 cup of sauce on top of the noodles. Place 1/2 of each of the onion, bell pepper, mushroom, turkey, cheese and black olives on the sauce, followed by another 1/2 cup of sauce. Cover the mixture with another layer of noodles and 1/2 cup of sauce. Follow with the remaining vegetables, meat and cheese and the remaining sauce. Cover the pan with aluminum foil and bake for 60 minutes or until the cheese is melted. Remove from oven and allow flavors to blend at least 15 minutes.

Serve warm.

Serves 3-5

October 13th <Saturday> Sunday 1805
The wife of Shabono our interpetr we find reconsiles all the Indians, as to our friendly intentions a woman with a party of men is a token of peace

William Clark

Smoked Turkey Salad

2 cups smoked turkey breast, diced

1 1/2 cups cooked rice

3/4 cup green bell pepper, diced

3/4 cup red onion, diced

1/2 cup salad dressing

1/2 cup sour cream

2 Tablespoons hot and spicy prepared mustard

4-5 fresh basil leaves, chopped

fresh ground black pepper to taste

Combine all ingredients and allow flavors to blend about 5 minutes.

May be served chilled.

Serves 3-5

October 19th Saturday 1805
the sight of This Indian woman, wife to one of our interprs. confirmed
those people of our friendly intentions, as no woman ever accompanies
a war party of Indians in this quarter--

William Clark

Poco con Pollo
(a little with chicken)

2 medium grilled chicken breasts, diced

1 small Portabella mushroom, diced

1/2 cup black olives, pitted and sliced

1/2 cup red onion, diced

2 10-ounce cans of enchilada sauce

10 ounces extra sharp cheddar cheese, shredded

8 small corn tortillas

Preheat oven to 325 degrees F. Place a small amount of sauce in the bottom of a 9x9-inch baking dish. Place 4 tortillas on the sauce and top with half of the chicken, mushroom, olives, onion and cheese; followed by a little more sauce. Place the remaining 4 tortillas on top, followed by the remaining chicken, vegetables, sauce and cheese. Bake for 20-25 minutes, uncovered.

Serve warm with your favorite green salad.

Serves 3

Friday 16th August 1805

Capt. Clark our Intrepter & wife walked on Shore and found a great nomber of fine berrys which is called Servis berrys. our Ints. wife gethered a pale full & gave them to the party at noon where we halted at a grove of cotton trees on L.S.

Joseph Whitehouse

125

Sage Grouse Pot

4 grouse breasts, chopped (substitute chicken)

2 cloves roasted garlic, minced

1 leek, carefully rinsed and chopped

1 carrot, peeled and chopped

1 large potato, peeled and diced

2 Tablespoons canola oil

2 teaspoons curry powder

1/2 teaspoon ground allspice

1 1-inch piece ginger, peeled and grated

1 cup coconut milk

1/4 teaspoon ground red pepper

In large soup pot, sauté grouse, garlic, leek, carrot and potato in oil until onions are translucent. Add curry, allspice and ginger stirring for another few minutes. Add the coconut milk and pepper. Simmer for 20 minutes or until potatoes and carrots are done.

Serve on a bed of rice.

Serves 2-3

Wednesday November the 20th 1805

one of the Indians had on a roab made of 2 Sea Otter Skins the fur of them were more butifull than any fur I had ever Seen both Capt. Lewis & my Self endeavored to purchase the roab with different articles   at length we precured it for a belt of blue beeds which the Squar- wife of our interpreter Shabono wore around her waste.

William Clark

Nut Butter Chicken Skewers

4 chicken breasts, cut lengthwise (long enough to skewer)

1 cup crunchy peanut butter

1/3 cup fresh cilantro, chopped

3/4 cup hot salsa

1/2 cup low sodium soy sauce

1/4 teaspoon liquid smoke

2 Tablespoons brown sugar, firmly packed

1 Tablespoon honey

1 Tablespoon sunflower nuts, unsalted and roasted

1/4 cup fresh lemon juice

1/2 teaspoon fresh ground black pepper

2 Tablespoons minced garlic

1 cup tomato juice

onion wedges

If using wooden skewers, soak them in water overnight to prevent burning on the grill. In medium bowl, combine all the ingredients except tomato juice. Add breasts and sauce to a 1-gallon sealable plastic bag. Refrigerate and marinate for at least 4 hours. Skewer meat alternating with onions and vegetables of your choice. Grill over medium heat, turning once, for 6-8 minutes until chicken is well done. While meat is grilling, pour remaining nut sauce into a medium saucepan. Stir in tomato juice. Bring to a slow boil over medium heat. Reduce heat to simmer until ready to serve skewers.

Serve skewers on a bed of rice topped with sauce.

Serves 4

Honey Bird Roast

3/4 cup soy sauce

1/4 cup chokecherry syrup

1/2 cup honey

1 clove garlic, minced

1/4 teaspoon fresh grated ginger

3 Tablespoons melted butter

2 Tablespoons apple cider vinegar

1/2 teaspoon ground allspice

3 chicken breasts cut lengthwise in slices (large enough to skewer)

1 teaspoon sesame seeds

red and green pepper wedges

onion wedges

If using wooden skewers, soak them in water overnight to prevent burning on the grill. Place all ingredients, except the chicken and sesame seeds, in a medium saucepan and bring to a boil over medium heat. Reduce heat to simmer for an additional 5 minutes. Allow marinade to cool completely. Pour marinade and chicken into a sealable plastic bag and refrigerate for at least 4 hours. Skewer meat with onions and red and green peppers. Grill over medium coals for 6 to 8 minutes turning once.

Serve with rice. Garnish with sesame seeds.

Serves 3-4

~ Sacagawea was allowed to vote on where to build winter camp. ~
(So was York, Clark's slave.)

November 24th Sunday 1805

Janey⁵ in favour of a place where there is plenty of Potas.

⁵A nickname for Sacagawea

William Clark

Creamed Pheasant With Wild Rice

1 pheasant, boned, cut in bite sized
    pieces (substitute chicken)

2 cloves garlic, minced

1 cup onion, chopped

1/4 cup red bell pepper, chopped

1 cup fresh mushrooms, chopped

1 8-ounce can sliced water chestnuts,
    drained and slivered

2 stalks celery, chopped

2 Tablespoons butter

2 Tablespoons canola oil

1/2 cup all-purpose white flour

2 cups chicken stock

1 teaspoon dried sweet basil leaves

1/4 teaspoon ground nutmeg

fresh ground black pepper to taste

1 cup cream

2 cups cheddar cheese, grated

3 cups steamed white rice

1 cup steamed wild rice

1/4 cup chopped hazelnuts

In a large cast iron skillet over medium heat, sauté pheasant, garlic, onion, bell pepper, mushrooms, chestnuts and celery in butter and oil until meat is done. Reduce heat to warm. In a medium saucepan over medium heat, stir stock into flour gradually. Add basil, nutmeg and pepper. Stir until mixture is thick. Stir in cream until blended. Remove sauce from heat and stir into meat mixture, incorporating the pan drippings. When heated through, pour over rices on serving platter.

Top with hazelnuts and cheese.

Serves 4-6

Baked Mushroom Chicken

4 large skinless, boneless chicken breasts

3/4 cup soy sauce

3/4 cup light brown sugar, firmly packed

2 Tablespoons raw unsalted sunflower nuts

2 Tablespoons canola oil

1/8 teaspoon dark sesame oil

1 Tablespoon fresh grated ginger

1/4 cup diced onion

fresh ground black pepper to taste

8 ounces fresh mushrooms, cleaned and sliced

Place chicken in an ovenproof baking dish. In a medium mixing bowl; combine remaining ingredients, except for the mushrooms to form a marinade. Pour marinade over the chicken and refrigerate for at least 2-3 hours, turning at least once. Preheat oven to 325 degrees F. and bake for 30 minutes. Add mushrooms, turn chicken breasts over and return to oven. Bake an additional 30 minutes, or until chicken is tender and cooked all the way through.

Serve with rice or potatoes. The marinade may be used as is or thickened and made into gravy.

Serves 4

Duck Breasts With Corn Dressing

1 1/2 pounds duck breast pieces, tenderized (substitute chicken or boneless pork)

2 Tablespoons canola oil

1 15-ounce can cream style corn

4 cups sourdough bread cubes

1 medium onion, diced

1 red bell pepper, diced

fresh ground black pepper to taste

1 cup grated Gruyere cheese

Preheat oven to 350 degrees F. Lightly salt and pepper the duck pieces and place them in the bottom of an ovenproof casserole. Combine remaining ingredients in a large mixing bowl and spread mixture evenly over the meat. Cover the casserole and bake for about 60 minutes, until the dressing is golden brown and dark around the edges. Remove from oven, take off lid and allow flavors to blend at least 10 minutes.

Serve with a green salad.

Serves 3-4

Saturday 30th of November 1805

The Squar gave me a piece of bread made of flour which She had reserved for her child and carefully Kept untill this time, which has unfortunately got wet, and a little Sour- this bread I eate with great Satisfaction, it being the only mouthfull I had tasted for Several months past.

William Clark

Spicy Garden Bird Pot

4 pheasant breasts, sliced (substitute 2 chicken breasts)

1/4 cup onion chopped

3 Tablespoons scallions, chopped

2 Tablespoons sun-dried tomatoes in oil, chopped

1/4 cup baby carrots, sliced

2 cloves garlic, minced

2 Tablespoons butter

1/4 cup shredded green cabbage

1 teaspoon fresh grated ginger

2 Tablespoons blue cheese

1/2 teaspoon red curry paste

3 Tablespoons sifted all-purpose white flour

1 14-ounce can coconut milk

4 cups cooked rice

1 cup cooked wild rice

slivered almonds

In large skillet over medium heat, sauté meat, onions, scallions, tomatoes, carrots and garlic in butter until meat is done. Add cabbage, ginger, blue cheese and curry paste tossing lightly. Reduce heat to low. In a separate bowl, stir coconut milk into flour until smooth. Add coconut mixture to meat mixture, stirring until mixture is thick. Mix rices on a platter. Spoon meat mixture over rice.

Top with slivered almonds.

Serves 3-4

December 3rd Tuesday 1805

The Squar Broke the two Shank bones of the Elk after the marrow was taken out, boiled them & extracted a Pint of Greese or tallow from them--

William Clark

Potato and Poultry Bake

Potatoes:
8 cups boiled potatoes, quartered then slightly mashed (with skins)

2 Tablespoons fresh dill, chopped

1 1/2 teaspoons minced roasted garlic

1/4 teaspoon salt

Chicken & Vegetable Mixture:
2 large chicken breasts, smoked and grilled

1 1/2 cups pumpkin, seeded, peeled, cut into 1-inch chunks and steamed

1/2 cup string beans, chopped and steamed

1 cup turnips, peeled, cut into 1-inch chunks and steamed

1 medium onion, chopped

1 teaspoon roasted garlic

1/2 teaspoon salt

fresh ground black pepper to taste

Sauce:
1 cup whole milk

1 Tablespoon corn starch

1/2 teaspoon chicken bouillon

Top:
2 Tablespoons butter

Preheat oven to 350 degrees F. Combine potato ingredients in a medium bowl. Set aside. In a large skillet, over medium heat, sauté the chicken and vegetable mixture. Reduce heat to low stirring occasionally. In a medium sauce pan, combine the sauce ingredients. Place over medium heat, stirring constantly until sauce is thick. Butter an 8 1/2x11-inch cake pan. Place 1/2 of the potato mixture in the bottom of the buttered pan. Next, layer the chicken and vegetable mixture then the sauce over that. Top with the rest of the potato mixture and dot with butter. Cover with foil and bake for 30 minutes.

Serves 5-7

Dilled Green Bean Potato Chowder With Eggs

4 cups water

5 medium potatoes, peeled and cubed

2 Tablespoons pickling spice, in a tea ball

1/2 teaspoon salt

2 cups string beans, julienne cut

3 Tablespoons fresh dill weed, minced

1 cup cream mixed with 2 Tablespoons sifted all-purpose white flour

4 eggs

apple cider vinegar to taste

In a large Dutch oven over medium heat, boil potatoes, salt, green beans, dill and pickling spice together until potatoes are done (about 20 minutes). Remove pickling spice and discard. Add cream mixture stirring constantly until thick. Drop eggs 1 by 1 carefully into chowder. After chowder starts to simmer again, carefully loosen eggs from bottom of pan. Simmer for 20 more minutes.

Serve with apple cider vinegar on the side.

Serves 4

December 25th Christmas 1805 Wednesday
we dried Some of our wet goods. I rcved a present of a Fleeshe Hoserey vest draws & Socks of Capt Lewis, pr. Mockerson of Whitehouse, a Small Indian basket of Guterich, & 2 Doz weasels tales of the Squar of Shabono

William Clark

"*Lewis and Clark on the Lower Columbia*"

Charles M. Russell — 1905, Opaque and transparent watercolor over graphite underdrawing on paper, 18 7/8" X 23 7/8"

Courtesy of Amon Carter Museum, Fort Worth, Texas

"Drying Salmon at the Dalles, Columbia River"
Paul Kane (1810-1871) — Watercolor on paper, 5 1/2" X 9 1/4"
Courtesy of Stark Museum of Art, Orange, Texas

From the... Water

Thursday November 21st 1805
The food of this nation is principally fish & roots the fish they precure from the river by the means of nets and gigs, and the Salmon which run up the Small branches together with what they collect drifted up on the Shores of the Sea coast near to where they live—

William Clark

Grilled Fish With Mustard Dill Chipotle Sauce

1/2 teaspoon salt

fresh ground black pepper to taste

1 pound fish fillets

1/2 cup chicken broth

2 teaspoons grainy mustard

1 teaspoon finely chopped fresh dill weed

1 teaspoon chipotle pepper in adobo sauce (finely chopped or sauce only)

2 Tablespoons cream cheese

1 scallion finely chopped

Salt and pepper fish and grill to taste. In a medium saucepan, combine broth, mustard, dill weed, chipotle and cream cheese. Heat over medium heat. Do not boil. When fish is ready to serve, pour sauce over each individual serving.

Garnish with chopped scallion.

Serves 4

January 1806, Tuesday 7th

The Indians, who live up there are of another nation, and call themselves the Callemex nation. They are a ferocious nation: one them was going kill one of our men, for his blanket; but was prevented by a squaw of the Chinook nation, who lives among them, and who raised an alarm.

Patrick Gass

Grilled Walleye Salad

Salad:

1 pound Walleye fillets, grilled and
    separated into chunks

4-6 dark green lettuce leaves

4-6 dark red lettuce leaves

4 ounces fresh spinach, stemmed

6 baby carrots, sliced thin

1/3 cup diced red onion

1/2 cup roasted sunflower nuts

1/2 cup golden raisins

1/2 pint (or more) grape tomatoes

1 Tablespoon fresh dill weed, minced

Dressing:

1 cup extra virgin olive oil

1/4 cup fresh lemon juice

2 teaspoons sugar

1 teaspoon kosher salt

2 cloves roasted garlic, minced

fresh ground black pepper to taste

Place all salad ingredients in a large serving bowl. In a small mixing bowl, combine all dressing ingredients and whisk vigorously. Pour over salad and toss lightly.

Serve immediately.

Serves 4-5

Grilled Catfish With Portabella Mushrooms and Peppers

11/2 pounds catfish fillets, grilled

2 Tablespoons extra virgin olive oil

1 medium white onion, diced

1/2 yellow bell pepper, julienne cut

1/2 red bell pepper, julienne cut

1/2 green bell pepper, julienne cut

2 medium Portabella mushrooms, cut in 1/2-inch thick slices

kosher salt

fresh ground black pepper to taste

1 Tablespoon each of:
   Worcestershire sauce
   soy sauce
   ketchup

juice from 1/2 lime

Place olive oil and onion in a skillet over medium low heat. When onions have started to soften, add peppers and mushrooms. Stir constantly to coat with oil and then add salt and pepper. When peppers and mushrooms have started to soften add sauces and ketchup. When vegetables are tender yet firm, remove skillet from heat, add lime juice and toss lightly. Allow flavors to blend for several minutes. Place mixture over warm grilled fillets and serve immediately.

Serve with rice or potatoes and your favorite salad.

Serves 3-4

Mushroom Stuffed Fish

2 Tablespoons butter

2 scallions, chopped

1/2 cup celery, chopped

1/2 cup mushrooms, chopped

2 Tablespoons mayonnaise

1 Tablespoon lemon juice

1 teaspoon stone ground mustard

2 ounces chopped pimento, drained

2 Tablespoons sunflower nuts, unsalted
and roasted

1 pound salmon fillets, grilled with salt
and pepper

Place butter, scallions, celery and mushrooms in a skillet over medium low heat. When mushrooms have started to soften add mayonnaise, lemon juice, mustard, pimento, sunflower nuts and mix. Remove from heat and allow flavors to blend for several minutes. Place mixture over warm grilled fillets and serve immediately.

Serves 3-4

Wednesday 9th July 1806
The Squar brought me a Plant the root of which the nativs eat. this root most resembles a Carrot in form and Size and Something of its colour, being of a pailer yellow than that of our Carrot, the Stem and leaf is much like the Common Carrot, and the taste not unlike. it is a native of moist land.--

William Clark

Salmon and Corn Salad

1 pound grilled salmon fillets, flaked

3 cups corn kernels, rinsed and drained

2 Tablespoons butter

2 Tablespoons pimento, diced

4 scallions, sliced

4 fresh dill sprigs, chopped

juice from 1 lemon

kosher salt to taste

fresh ground black pepper to taste

Place salmon in a serving bowl. Lightly sauté the corn in the butter and add to bowl. Add remaining ingredients and toss lightly. Allow flavors to blend 5 minutes.

Serve warm.

Serves 3

Monday April 28th 1806

We found a Sho Sho ne woman, prisoner among those people by means of whome and Sah-cah gah-weah, Shabono's wife we found means of Converceing with the Wallahwallârs. we Conversed with them for Several hours and fully Satisfy all their enquiries with respect to our Selves and the Object of our pursute.

William Clark

142

Spiced Shrimp Roast

Marinade:
12-14 large shrimp shelled and deveined
1 Tablespoon extra virgin olive oil
2 teaspoons seafood seasoning
1 teaspoon minced garlic

Sauce Mixture:
1/4 cup salad dressing
1 teaspoon lemon juice
1 Tablespoon sweet pickle relish

Combine marinade ingredients in a sealable plastic bag. Refrigerate for about an hour. Mix the sauce ingredients in a small bowl and refrigerate. Grill shrimp over hot coals for about 3-5 minutes each side. Do not overcook.

Serve on platter with sauce on the side.

Serves 3-4

Monday April 28th 1806
one of their party who made himself the most Conspicious Charecter in the dance and Songs, we were told was a Medesene man & Could foretell things. that he had told of our Comeing into their Country and was now about to Consult his God the moon if what we Said was the truth &c.&c.

William Clark

Fish Bake

1/4 cup mayonnaise

1/4 cup sour cream

1 Tablespoon white balsamic vinegar

1/2 teaspoon dry mustard

dash hot pepper sauce

2 scallions, finely chopped

1 clove garlic, minced

1/2 teaspoon seafood seasoning

2-3 pounds white fish fillets, cut into 8 ounce serving sizes

Preheat oven to 350 degrees F. Combine all ingredients except fish, in a medium bowl. Place fish in a 8 1/2x11-inch ovenproof baking dish. Spread sauce over fish and bake for 20 minutes or until fish is done.

Serves 4

Sunday 11th May 1806

Some little rain last night. we were Crouded in the Lodge with Indians who continued all night and this morning Great numbers were around us. The One Eyed Chief Yoom-park-kar-tim arived and we gave him a medal of the Small Size and Spoke to the Indians through a Snake boy Shabono and his wife. we informed them who we were, where we Came from & our intentions towards them, which pleased them very much.

William Clark

Trout Pot

2 trout fillets, chopped (substitute any fish fillets)

2 cloves garlic, minced

1 leek, carefully rinsed and chopped

1 carrot, peeled and chopped

1 turnip, peeled and diced

2 Tablespoons butter

1/4 teaspoon red curry paste

1 cup coconut milk

1/2 cup broccoli florets

1 stalk celery, chopped

1/4 cup cheddar cheese, grated

In large soup pot, sauté fish, garlic, leek, carrot and turnip in butter until onions are translucent. Add curry paste stirring for another few minutes. Add the coconut milk and broccoli. Simmer for 20 minutes or until turnips and carrots are done. Stir in celery and cheddar cheese.

Serve on a bed of rice.

Serves 3-4

Crispy Potato Walleye Fillets

3 medium red potatoes, soaked in water overnight
4 large thin walleye fillets
coarse ground prepared mustard
fresh ground black pepper to taste
oil and butter for frying

Drain water off of potatoes and peel. Using a medium grater, grate potatoes into a bowl.

Spread a thin layer of mustard on each side of the fillets and add pepper to taste. Press a handful of grated potatoes on both sides of each fillet. Fry immediately in a heavy skillet with equal amounts of oil and butter over medium low heat, turning when potatoes are brown and crispy. When done, remove from heat and serve immediately.

Serves 4

Friday May 16th 1806
Sahcargarmeah geathered a quantity of the roots of a speceis of fennel which we found very agreeable food, the flavor of this root is not unlike annis seed...

Meriwether Lewis

Anna's Panfried Walleye Fillets

1 1/2-2 pounds fresh walleye fillets

kosher salt to taste

fresh ground black pepper to taste

3/4 cup sifted all-purpose white flour

3/4 cup yellow cornmeal

1 small red onion, diced

butter and corn oil for frying

fresh dill weed, minced

lettuce leaves

lemon wedges

Salt and pepper each fillet. Combine flour and cornmeal with a little more salt and pepper in a large plastic bag. Place fillets in bag and shake vigorously. Place the onion along with equal amounts of oil and butter in a large skillet over medium low heat. Shake the excess flour off of each fillet, add to skillet and fry until golden brown. Turn fillets and fry until other side is brown, adding more butter and oil as needed. Arrange lettuce leaves on a serving platter and place fried fillets on top of the lettuce. Top with minced dill and arrange lemon wedges around edges of platter.

Serve with your favorite bread and salad.

Serves 3-4

Drowned Catfish

4 large, thin catfish fillets

2 cups buttermilk (as needed)

kosher salt to taste

fresh ground black pepper to taste

3/4 cup yellow cornmeal

3/4 cup sifted all-purpose white flour

1 teaspoon onion powder

1 teaspoon dried dillweed

butter and canola oil for frying

Salt and pepper each fillet and place in a single layer in a flat bottomed dish. Add buttermilk to cover. Marinate in the refrigerator for at least 30 minutes, turning once. Remove fillets from marinade and blot dry with paper towels. Discard liquid. Combine salt, pepper, cornmeal, flour, onion powder and dill weed in a large plastic bag and shake until well mixed. Add fillets, one at a time, and shake until well coated. Shake off excess coating mixture and sauté fillets in oil and butter in a large heavy skillet over medium heat. Turn after the first side is crispy and golden brown and fry until the other side is equally done.

Serve warm with *Tartar Sauce* (see recipe page 176), a green salad and corn bread.

Serves 4

Fish Chowder

1 Tablespoon butter

1 medium onion, chopped

1 stalk celery, chopped

1 carrot, peeled and chopped

1 cup ham, chopped

1 cup chicken broth

1 cup water

1 cup clam juice

1 large potato, peeled and chopped

1/2 cup asparagus, chopped

1 bay leaf

1 pound fish fillets, chopped

1/2 cup chopped cooked spinach

1/2 cup sour cream

3 Tablespoons all-purpose white flour

In a large Dutch oven, sauté onion, celery and carrot with butter until onion is translucent and carrot is bright orange. Add all the rest of the ingredients except the spinach, sour cream and flour. Simmer until vegetables are tender. Add spinach, sour cream and flour, reheat and serve.

Serves 6-8

Shrimp and Pheasant Pasta

1 medium onion halved, then sliced

1 teaspoon garlic, minced

2 Tablespoons butter

8 ounces mushrooms, sliced

1/2 teaspoon cayenne, ground

1 teaspoon seafood seasoning

8 ounces cream cheese

5 Tablespoons milk

fresh ground black pepper to taste

2 pheasant breasts (substitute chicken), grilled and seasoned with Cajun spice, sliced

8 large shrimp, shelled, deveined, grilled and seasoned with Cajun spice

fettuccini pasta, cooked and tossed with butter (enough to serve 4)

1/2 tomato, chopped

2 scallions, chopped

In a large sauté pan, sauté onion and garlic in butter until onion is translucent. Add mushrooms and sauté an additional minute. Reduce heat to low. Add spices and cream cheese; stirring occasionally until cheese is melted. Gradually add milk to achieve desired consistency. As sauce sets, you may need to add more milk.

On each plate: layer noodles, then 1/4 of the breast meat and 2 shrimp, followed by 1/4 of the sauce.

Garnish with chopped scallions, chopped tomatoes and fresh ground black pepper.

Serves 4

Crab and Chinook Salmon Wrapped in Corn Husks

8 large dried corn husks

1 can (4 1/4-ounce) of crab meat, drained

1 Tablespoon lemon zest, minced

1 teaspoon seafood seasoning

1 scallion, chopped diagonally

2 teaspoons roasted garlic, minced

1 1/2 Tablespoons fresh dill, minced

2 6-ounce salmon steaks

1 Tablespoon corn oil

salt to taste

fresh ground black pepper to taste

Soak dried corn husks in cold water for 20 minutes prior to use. Preheat grill on high. In a medium mixing bowl, add crab, zest, seafood seasoning, onions, garlic, and fresh dill. Oil grilling basket or coat with butter flavored non-stick cooking spray. Remove 2 corn husks from water, do not dry. Place steak on first layer of corn husk. Liberally coat steak with corn oil, salt and pepper. Spread crab mixture over steak. Cover with 2 corn husks. Repeat process for remaining steaks. Close grilling basket. Turn grill to low. Grill four minutes each side. Salmon is done when flaky.

Serve with crisp salad and rice.

Serves 2

Grilled Walleye With Creamy Dilled Lemon Sauce

2 pounds fish fillets, seasoned with salt and pepper

3/4 cup chicken broth

1 Tablespoon finely chopped fresh dill weed

4 Tablespoons cream cheese

1/2 teaspoon minced roasted garlic

1 teaspoon lemon zest

1/2 teaspoon fresh ground black pepper

1/4 cup chopped scallion

Grill fish. In a medium sauce pan, combine stock, dill weed, cream cheese, garlic, zest and pepper. Heat over medium heat. Do not boil. Pour sauce over fish and serve.

Garnish with chopped scallion.

Serves 4

Friday 16th May 1806
Shabonos Squar gatherd a quantity of fenel roots which we find very paleatiable and nurishing food. the Onion we also find in abundance and boil it with our meat.

William Clark

Chinook Lodge - Mount Hood in the distance

"A Chinook Traveling Lodge With View of Mount Hood"
Paul Kane (1810-1871) — 1847, Watercolor on paper, 5 1/2" X 9"
Courtesy of Stark Museum of Art, Orange, Texas

"Visitors at Fort Clatsop"
John F. Clymer — 1978, Oil
Courtesy of Clymer Museum & Gallery, Ellensburg, Washington

Sweet Enough

Thursday February 20th 1806

This forenoon we were visited by Tah-cum a principal chief of the Chinooks and 25 men of his nation. we had never Seen this Chief before he is a good looking man of about 50 years of age reather larger in Statue than most of his nation; as he came on a friendly visit we gave himself and party something to eate and plyed them plenty fully with Smoke. we gave this chief a small Medal with which he Seamed much pleased. in the evening at Sunset we desired them to depart as is our custom and Close our gates. we never Suffer parties of Such numbers to remain within the Fort all night; for not withstanding their apparent friendly disposition, their great averis and hope of plunder might induce them to be treacherous.

William Clark

Juneberry Dumplings

Dumplings:

2 cups sifted all-purpose white flour

4 teaspoons baking powder

2 Tablespoons granulated white sugar

1/2 teaspoon salt

1/2 cup butter

3/4 cup milk

Berry Sauce:

1 cup granulated white sugar

1 cup water

3 Tablespoons cornstarch

1 teaspoon lemon zest

1/4 teaspoon ground nutmeg

1 pound ripe juneberries (substitute blueberries or black raspberries)

1/2 teaspoon vanilla extract

Preheat oven to 350 degrees F. In a medium bowl, combine flour, baking powder, sugar and salt. Cut in butter until mixture is crumbly. Gently stir in milk. Do not over mix. Set aside. In a saucepan add sugar, water, cornstarch, zest and nutmeg. Stir until mixture is smooth. Bring to boil over medium heat stirring constantly until mixture is thick. Remove from heat and gently stir in berries. Pour berry mixture into an 8 1/2x11-inch cake pan. Spoon dumplings over top. Bake for 20 minutes or until dumplings are done.

Serve with cream or ice cream.

Yield: 12 pieces

Sunday May 18th 1806.

our indian woman was busily engaged today in laying in a store of the fennel roots for the Rocky mountains. these are called by the Shoshones year-pah.

Meriwether Lewis

Oatmeal Cookies

4 cups sifted all-purpose white flour

2 teaspoons baking soda

2 teaspoons salt

1/2 cup butter, softened

1 1/2 cups canola oil

2 cups granulated white sugar

2 cups brown sugar, firmly packed

1 1/2 cups old fashioned rolled oats

4 eggs, slightly beaten

4 cups rice crispies

2 teaspoons vanilla extract

2 cups raisins

Preheat oven to 350 degrees F. Combine flour and baking soda in a bowl. In a separate bowl, combine remaining ingredients and mix until smooth and creamy. Slowly add dry mixture to liquid until thoroughly blended. Use two spoons to drop cookie dough onto oiled baking sheets. Bake for 10-12 minutes.

Yield: about 4 dozen cookies, depending on size

Colter's Chokecherry Spritzer

12 ounces chokecherry syrup (substitute black cherry syrup)

1 teaspoon lime zest, very finely minced

1 cup whole milk

1/2 cup pasteurized egg product

1 1/2 cups club soda

1 teaspoon vanilla extract

8 ice cubes

Combine all ingredients in a blender.

Serve over cracked ice.

Serves 4-6

Sunday 18th May 1806

The Squar wife to Shabono busied her Self gathering the roots of the fenel Called by the Snake Indians Year-pah for the purpose of drying to eate on the Rocky mountains. those roots are very paliatiable either fresh rosted boiled or dried and generally between the Size of a quill and that of a mans fingar and about the length of the latter.

William Clark

Grandpa's Apple Butter

6 large tart apples, peeled, quartered
  and cored

1/2 cup cold water

1 stick cinnamon

1/2 cup granulated white sugar

dash fresh ground black pepper

1/4 teaspoon ground cloves

1/4 teaspoon ground allspice

1/2 teaspoon vanilla extract

1/2 teaspoon butter flavoring

In a non-reactive saucepan add apples, water and cinnamon. Bring to a boil and then reduce heat. Cook for 20 minutes until mixture is reduced by half. Stir gently. Add sugar, pepper, cloves, allspice, vanilla and butter flavoring. Return to a boil and reduce heat. Cook until desired thickness is attained, approximately 25 minutes. Place in sterilized jars and refrigerate.

Serve chilled.

Yield: 4 cups

Sunday 18th May 1806
LaPage took a Salmon from an Eagle at a Short distance below our Camp. this is induces us to believe that the Salmon is in this river and most probably will be here in great numbers in the Course of a fiew days.

William Clark

Pumpkin Nut Bake

1 9-inch pie shell

<u>Pumpkin Filling:</u>

1 15-ounce can pumpkin

1/2 teaspoon ground cinnamon

1/4 teaspoon ground mace

1/4 teaspoon ground nutmeg

1 egg, beaten

1/3 cup granulated white sugar

<u>Topping:</u>

2 eggs, beaten

1/2 cup granulated white sugar

1/2 teaspoon vanilla extract

2/3 cup maple syrup

3 Tablespoons butter, softened

1/2 cup pecans, chopped

1/2 cup hazelnuts, chopped

Preheat oven to 350 degrees F. Combine filling ingredients in a bowl. Pour into pie crust. In a separate bowl combine the topping ingredients. Distribute over pumpkin mixture. Bake for 50 minutes or until knife inserted in the middle comes out clean.

Serve with ice cream.

Yield: 12 pieces

Thursday May 22ed 1806.

Charbono's Child is very ill this evening; he is cuting teeth, and for several days past has had a violent lax, which having suddonly stoped he was attacked with a high fever and his neck and throat are much swolen this evening.

Meriwether Lewis

Berry Pastry

1 cup granulated white sugar

1/4 cup cornstarch

1 cup water

1 teaspoon lemon juice

1/4 teaspoon ground cinnamon

1/4 teaspoon ground nutmeg

1/4 teaspoon ground mace

2 cups frozen blueberries

6 puff pastry shells

In a non-reactive saucepan combine sugar and cornstarch. Add water, lemon juice and spices. Bring to a boil and reduce heat. Stir constantly until thick. Gently stir in berries and set aside. Prepare shells according to package instructions. Fill shells with berry mixture and top with whipped cream.

Serves 6

Thursday 22nd May 1806

Shabonoes Son a Small child is, dangerously ill. his jaw and throat is much Swelled. we apply a poltice of Onions. after giveing him Some creem of tarter &c.

William Clark

Sourdough Currant Cake

1/2 cup butter

1 1/2 cups brown sugar, firmly packed

1 teaspoon vanilla extract

2 cups *Sourdough Starter* (see recipe page 54)

2 teaspoons baking soda

2 cups sifted all-purpose white flour

1/2 teaspoon ground cinnamon

1/2 teaspoon ground cloves

1/2 teaspoon ground allspice

1/2 teaspoon ground nutmeg

1/4 teaspoon salt

dash of fresh ground black pepper

3/4 cup dried currants

1/2 cup walnuts, coarsely chopped

Preheat oven to 350 degrees F. Cream butter, sugar and vanilla. In a separate bowl add soda to sourdough starter. Stir well. Sift flour, cinnamon, cloves, allspice, nutmeg, salt and pepper. Gently fold all ingredients together. Add batter to pan. Place in oven and bake for 35 minutes.

Top with *Missouri River Maplenut Frosting* (see recipe page 163).

Yield: 1 cake

Wednesday June 25th 1806
here we halted and dined and our guides overtook us. at this place the squaw Collected a parcel of roots of which the Shoshones Eat. it is a Small knob root a good deel in flavour and Consistency like the Jerusolem artichoke.

William Clark

Missouri River Maplenut Frosting

1 8-ounce package cream cheese, softened

2 Tablespoons butter

1 Tablespoon maple syrup

2 teaspoons vanilla extract

1/4 teaspoon butter flavoring

1/4 teaspoon maple flavoring

pinch of salt

1 cup powdered sugar, sifted

1 cup walnuts, chopped

In a medium mixing bowl combine cream cheese and butter. Mix until smooth. Add syrup, vanilla extract, butter flavoring, maple flavoring and salt. Blend in powdered sugar. Use on your favorite cake or pastries.

Garnish with walnuts.

Yield: about 2 cups

Tuesday July 1st 1806

...Capt C. with the remaining ten including Charbono and York will proceed to the Yellowstone river at it's nearest approach to the three forks of the missouri, here he will build a canoe and descend the Yellowstone river with Charbono the indian woman, his servant York and five others to the missouri where should he arrive first he will wait my arrival.

Meriwether Lewis

163

Pumpkin Patch Dessert

Crust:

1 cup old fashioned rolled oats

3/4 cup granulated white sugar

1/2 cup butter

3/4 cup sifted all-purpose white flour

1/4 cup coarsely chopped hazelnuts

Filling:

2 8-ounce packages cream cheese, softened

1/3 cup brown sugar, firmly packed

1 teaspoon vanilla extract

1/4 teaspoon salt

Filling *(continued)*:

4 eggs, beaten

1/2 cup maple syrup

1 teaspoon ground cinnamon

1/4 teaspoon ground cloves

1/4 teaspoon ground cardamom

1/4 teaspoon ground allspice

1/4 teaspoon ground mace

1 15-ounce can pumpkin

1 Tablespoon sifted all-purpose white flour

Preheat oven to 350 degrees F. Place oatmeal in blender and coarsely grind. In a large mixing bowl, blend butter and white sugar until smooth. Add oatmeal, flour and nuts. Stir until crumbly. Press into an 8 1/2x11-inch pan and bake 18 minutes. In a medium sized bowl, combine cream cheese and brown sugar. Add vanilla and salt. Stir in eggs, a little at a time. Add remaining ingredients and mix well. Pour into baked crust and bake an additional 45 minutes or until knife inserted in center comes out clean.

Top with whipped cream, if desired.

Serves 12

"Burry" Glaze Cheese Cake

Crust:
1 3/4 cups graham cracker crumbs
1/4 cup chopped hazelnuts
1/2 teaspoon ground cinnamon
1/2 teaspoon lemon extract
1/3 cup melted butter

Filling:
32 ounces cream cheese, softened
12 ounces sour cream
1/2 teaspoon vanilla extract
1/2 teaspoon almond extract
1 teaspoon lemon zest
1 3/4 cups granulated white sugar
1/4 cup sifted all-purpose white flour
1/4 teaspoon kosher salt
5 eggs

Glaze:
1 cup granulated white sugar
1/4 cup cornstarch
1 cup water
1 teaspoon lemon juice
1/4 teaspoon ground cinnamon
1/4 teaspoon ground nutmeg
1/4 teaspoon ground mace
2 cups blackberries

Preheat oven to 400 degrees F. Combine crust ingredients in a bowl and press into the bottom of a buttered spring form pan. In a large mixing bowl, combine cheese, sour cream, extracts and zest. Beat until smooth and creamy. Add sugar, flour and salt. Beat until grainy texture disappears and filling is smooth. Add eggs, one at a time, mixing well between each one. Pour filling over crust and spread evenly. Bake for 15 minutes at 400 degrees F., then reduce heat to 300 degrees F. and bake for 60 minutes or until a knife inserted comes out clean. In a saucepan, combine the glaze ingredients. Cook over medium heat stirring constantly until glaze is thick. Set aside and keep warm.

Carefully remove cheesecake from oven and allow to cool undisturbed for one hour. Loosen sides carefully with a knife and release spring form.

Top individual pieces with glaze.

Yield: 12 pieces

Molasses Cookies

2 1/2 cups sifted all-purpose white flour

1 teaspoon baking soda

1/2 cup butter, softened

1 cup molasses

1 Tablespoon brown sugar, firmly packed

3 Tablespoons buttermilk

Preheat oven to 325 degrees F. Combine flour and baking soda in a bowl. In a separate bowl, combine remaining ingredients and mix until smooth and creamy. Slowly add dry mixture to liquid until thoroughly blended. Use two spoons to drop cookie dough onto oiled baking sheets. Slightly flatten cookies with the bottom of a glass dipped in water and sprinkle tops with a little coarse sugar. Bake for 12-15 minutes.

Yield: about 3 dozen cookies, depending on size

Tuesday July 1st 1806

Sergt Pryor with two other men are to proceed with the horses by land to the Mandans and thence to the British posts on the Assinniboin with a letter to Mr. Heney [NB: Haney] whom we wish to engage to <procure> prevail on the Sioux Chefs to join us on the Missouri,...

Meriwether Lewis

Cream Currant Bars

Crust and Topping:

1 cup butter

1 cup brown sugar, firmly packed

1/4 teaspoon butter flavoring

1 teaspoon baking soda

1 3/4 cups all-purpose white flour

1 3/4 cups old fashioned rolled oats

1/4 cup hazelnuts, crushed

Filling:

3 egg yolks

1 1/2 cups sour cream (reduced fat)

1/2 cup granulated white sugar

1/2 cup brown sugar, firmly packed

2 1/2 Tablespoons cornstarch

1 teaspoon vanilla extract

1/4 teaspoon ground nutmeg

2 cups fresh currants (substitute blueberries)

Preheat oven to 350 degrees F. In a bowl, cream together butter and brown sugar. Add butter flavoring, soda, flour, oatmeal and nuts. Pour half this mixture into a 9x13-inch cake pan and bake 7 minutes. Meanwhile, mix egg yolks, sour cream, sugars and cornstarch in a medium sauce pan. Bring to a boil over medium heat, stirring constantly. Remove from heat and carefully stir in the vanilla, nutmeg and currants. Pour filling on bottom crust. Crumble remaining oatmeal mixture over top of filling and return to oven. Bake an additional 30 minutes until topping is brown.

Yield: about 12 pieces

Berry Bread Pudding with Maple Sauce

Sauce:

1 cup heavy cream

3 large egg yolks

1/4 cup maple sugar *(Substitute 1/4 cup firmly packed brown sugar and 1/8 teaspoon maple flavoring.)*

pinch of salt

Bread Pudding:

4 large eggs

1 cup granulated white sugar

1/2 cup honey

1/2 teaspoon ground cinnamon

1/4 teaspoon ground nutmeg

1/2 teaspoon salt

3 cups heavy cream

6 cups cubed day-old sourdough bread, crusts removed

3/4 cup raspberries

3/4 cup blackberries

Combine sauce ingredients in a small saucepan. Bring to boil over medium heat stirring constantly. Remove from heat and place pan in ice water to cool. Preheat oven to 325 degrees F. In a large bowl, mix the eggs, sugar, honey, spices, salt and cream. Stir in the bread and let set for about 20 minutes. Pour bread mixture into a buttered 9x13-inch cake pan. Carefully fold in berries. Cover tightly with foil and bake for 40-50 minutes. Let cool.

Cut and serve with sauce over individual servings.

Serves 12

Old Fashioned Butterscotch Sauce

1/2 cup butter
1 cup granulated white sugar
1/2 cup brown sugar, firmly packed
1/2 cup heavy cream
pinch of salt

Combine sauce ingredients in a medium saucepan. Over medium heat, stirring constantly, bring sauce to rolling boil. Remove from heat and allow to cool slightly.

Serve warm over ice cream or cake.

Yield: about 2 cups

Sunday 6th July 1806
the Indian woman wife to Shabono informed me that she had been in this plain frequently and knew it well that the Creek which we decended was a branch of Wisdom river and when we assended the higher part of the plain we would discover a gap in the mountains in our direction to the Canoes, and when we arived at that gap we would See a high point of a mountain covered with snow in our direction to the canoes.

William Clark

Thursday 17th July 1806

I Saw in one of those Small bottoms which I passed this evening an Indian fort which appears to have been built last Summer. this fort was built of logs and bark. the logs was put up very Closely [NB: ends supporting each other] capping on each other about 5 feet [NB: high] and Closely chinked. around which bark was Set up on end so as to Cover the Logs. the enterance was also guarded by a work on each Side of it and faceing the river. this work is about 50 feet Diameter & nearly round. the Squaw informs me that when the war parties [NB: of Minnits Crows &, who fight Shoshonees] find themselves pursued they make those forts to defend themselves in from the pursuers whose Superior numbers might other wise over power them and cut them off without receiveing much injurey on hors back &c.

William Clark

"Scene on the Columbia River"
John Mix Stanley — ca. 1852, Oil on canvas, 17 1/8" X 21 1/8"
Courtesy of Amon Carter Museum, Fort Worth, Texas

"Sacajewea by the Big Water"
John F. Clymer — 1974, Oil
Courtesy of Clymer Museum & Gallery, Ellensburg, Washington

Everything Else

Monday January 6th 1806

Capt Clark set out after an early breakfast with the party in two canoes as had been concerted the last evening; Charbono and his Indian woman were also of the party; the Indian woman was very impotunate to be permitted to go, and was therefore indulged; she observed that she had traveled a long way with us to see the great waters, and that now that monstrous fish was also to be seen, she thought it very hard she could not be permitted to see either (she had never yet been to the Ocean).

Meriwether Lewis

Melon Salsa

1 1/4 cups watermelon, seeded and diced

1 1/4 cups cantaloupe, diced

1 jalapeno pepper, seeded and diced

1 teaspoon fresh mint, minced

1 1/2 teaspoons granulated white sugar

1 Tablespoon lemon or lime juice

Combine ingredients in a bowl and allow flavors to blend for 15 minutes.

Serve with your favorite grilled meat or poultry.

Yield: about 2 1/2 cups

Friday 25th July 1806

This rock which I shall Call Pompy's Tower is 200 feet high and 400 paces in secumphrance and only axcessable on one Side which is from the N.E the other parts of it being a perpendicular Clift of lightish Coloured gritty rock on the top there is a tolerable Soil of about 5 or 6 feet thick Covered with Short grass. The Indians have made 2 piles of Stone on the top of this Tower. The nativs have ingraved on the face of this rock the figures of animals &c. near which I marked my name and the day of the month & year.

William Clark

Jalapeno Mint Ranch Dressing

1/4 cup buttermilk

1/2 cup sour cream

1/2 cup mayonnaise

1/4 cup cucumbers, peeled, seeded and diced

2 teaspoons jalapeno pepper, minced

2 teaspoons fresh mint, finely minced

2 cloves roasted garlic, minced

1 Tablespoon extra virgin olive oil

1 teaspoon lemon zest

1 Tablespoon blue cheese

2 Tablespoons Parmesan cheese

1 teaspoon fresh ground black pepper

1/2 teaspoon kosher salt

1/4 teaspoon celery seed

1/4 cup bread crumbs

In a blender combine buttermilk, sour cream and mayonnaise. Blend until smooth. Add remaining ingredients and blend. Store in a covered container in the refrigerator overnight to allow flavors to blend. Serve over green leaf lettuce with grated carrots, shredded red cabbage, red onion, tomatoes and a peeled, seeded and diced cucumber.

Garnish with croutons and sunflower nuts.

Yield: 2 cups

Tartar Sauce

4 Tablespoons mayonnaise

2 Tablespoons sweet pickle relish

1 Tablespoon coarse ground prepared mustard

1 teaspoon cream of tartar

1/2 teaspoon dried dill weed

1 Tablespoon very finely diced red onion or shallot

Combine all ingredients in a small bowl and stir until well blended. Cover bowl and chill for 20 minutes. Serve with your favorite fish or seafood. Also makes a unique spread for sandwiches.

Yield: about 1/2 cup

Creamy Mustard Sauce

1/2 cup heavy cream

1 1/2 Tablespoons prepared honey dijon mustard

1/4 teaspoon hot pepper sauce

1 teaspoon lemon juice

Whisk all ingredients together and simmer in a sauce pan for about 10 minutes, stirring frequently.

Serve with your favorite fritters or patties.

Yield: about 1/2 cup

Wednesday 4th August 1806
The Child of Shabono has been So much bitten by the Musquetor that his face is much puffed up & Swelled.

William Clark

Chipotle Ranch Dressing

1/2 cup buttermilk

1/2 cup sour cream

1/2 cup mayonnaise

2 Tablespoons Parmesan cheese

1 Tablespoon extra virgin olive oil

1 teaspoon fresh ground black pepper

1 teaspoon minced roasted garlic

1/2 teaspoon dry mustard

1/2 teaspoon kosher salt

1/4 teaspoon celery seed

1/4 teaspoon ground sweet Hungarian paprika

Blend all ingredients together. Chill for 1 hour before serving. Store unused portions in a sealed container in the refrigerator.

Servce with your favorite fritters or patties or as a dressing over a bed of mixed greens.

Yield: 2 cups

Monday 9th August 1806

The Squar brought me a [NB: 1800 Miles up the Missouri I found a] large and well favoured Goose berry of a rich Crimsin Colour, and deep purple berry of the large Cherry of the Current Speces which is common on this river as low as the Mandans, the engagees Call it the Indian Current.

William Clark

Notes:

Sunday 8th August 1806

at 8 A.M. Sergt. N. Pryor Shannon, hall & Windsor Came down the river in two Canoes made of Buffalow Skins. Sergt. Pryor informed me that the Second night after he parted with me on the river Rochejhone he arived about 4 P M on the banks of a large Creek which contained no running water. he halted to let the horses graze dureing which time a heavy Shower of rain raised the Creek so high that Several horses which had Stragled across the Channel of this Creek was obliged to Swim back. here he deturmined to Continue all night it being in good food for the horses. In the morning he could See no horses. in lookg about their Camp they discovered Several tracks within 100 paces of their Camp, which they pursued found where they had Caught and drove off all the horses. they prosued on five miles the Indians there divided into two parties. they Continued in pursute of the largest party five miles further finding that there was not the Smallest Chance of overtaking them, they returned to their Camp and packed up their baggage on their backs and Steared N.E. course to the River Rochejhone which they Struck at pompys Tower, there they killed a Buffalow Bull and made a Canoe in the form and shape of the mandans & Ricares

William Clark

180

"Arrival of Sergeant Pryor"
John F. Clymer — 1975, Oil
Courtesy of Clymer Museum & Gallery, Ellensburg, Washington

"Captain Clark Gangue of Buffalo"
John F. Clymer — 1976, Oil
Courtesy of Clymer Museum & Gallery, Ellensburg, Washington

Sunday 1st of August 1806.

at 2 P.M. I was obliged to land to let the Buffalow Cross over. not withstanding an island of half a mile in width over which this gangue of Buffalow had to pass and the Chanel of the river on each Side nearly 1/4 of a mile in width, this gangue of Buffalow was entirely across and as thick as they could swim. the Chanel on the Side of the island the went into the river was crouded with those animals for 1/2 an hour. [NB: I was obliged to lay to for an hour] the other Side of the island for more than 3/4 of an hour. I took 4 of the men and killed 4 fat Cows for their fat and what portion of their flesh the Small Canoes Could Carry that which we had killed a few days ago being nearly Spoiled from the wet weather. encamped on an Island Close to the Lard Shore. two gangues of Buffalow Crossed a little below us, as noumerous as the first.

William Clark

Saturday 17th of August 1806

we also took our leave of T. Chabono, his Snake Indian wife and their Son Child who had accompained us on our rout to the pacific Ocean in the Capacity of interpreter and interpretes. T. Chabono wished much to accompany us in the Said Capacity if <he> we could have provailed the Menetarre Chiefs to dcend the river with us to the U. States, but as none of those chiefs of whoes <set out> language he was Conversent would accompany us, his Services were no longer of use to the U'States and he was therefore discharged and paid up.   we offered to convey him down to the Illinois if he Chose to go, he declined proceeding on at present, observing that he had no acquaintance or prospects of makeing a liveing below, and must continue to live in the way that he had done. I offered to take his little Son a butifull promising Child who is 19 months old to which they both himself & wife wer willing provided the Child had been weened.   they observed that in one year the boy would be Sufficiently old to leave his mother & he would then take him to me if I would be so freindly as to raise the Child for him in Such a manner as I thought proper, to which I agreeed &c.--

William Clark

"Sun Worship in Montana"

Charles M. Russell — 1907, Opaque and transparent watercolor over graphite underdrawing on paper,
22 3/8" X 17 1/2" Courtesy of Amon Carter Museum, Fort Worth, Texas

Great Gift Ideas!

...birthdays, Christmas, anniversaries or just because _you_ deserve something special!

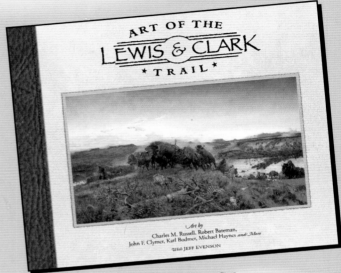

ART OF THE
LEWIS & CLARK
★ TRAIL ★

Art by
Charles M. Russell, Robert Bateman,
John F. Clymer, Karl Bodmer, Michael Haynes _and More_
With JEFF EVENSON

Experience the Journey!

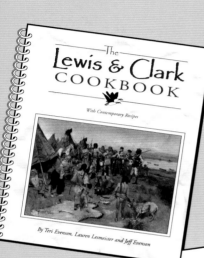

The
Lewis & Clark
COOKBOOK

With Contemporary Recipes

By Teri Evenson, Lauren Lesmeister and Jeff Evenson

Explore the Flavors!

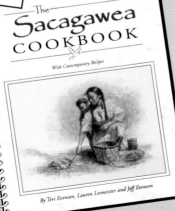

The
Sacagawea
COOKBOOK

With Contemporary Recipes

By Teri Evenson, Lauren Lesmeister and Jeff Evenson

Whisper'n Waters Order Blank

QTY			Price
	The Sacagawea Cookbook, $19.95 each	$	
	The Lewis and Clark Cookbook, $19.95 each	$	
	Art of the Lewis & Clark Trail , $42.95 each	$	
	Add $3.95 *per order* for shipping and handling	$	
	Sub Total	$	
	ND Residents, add 6% sales tax	$	
	TOTAL	$	

Name: _____

Address: _____

City: _____ State:_____ Zip:_____

Telephone: _____ E-mail:_____

Credit Card/Acct. #: _____ Exp. Date:_____

Signature: _____

Send completed order form with payment to:

Whisper'n WATERS

Whisper'n Waters, Inc.
328 Lunar Lane
Bismarck, ND 58503

VISA and MasterCard are welcome. Phone orders call: 1-888-282-7693 or fax: (701) 223-4259

Our cookbooks make a great gift for friends and family!

Gift orders mailed to:

Name: _____

Address: _____

City: _____ State:_____ Zip:_____

Gift Message: _____

Name: _____

Address: _____

City: _____ State:_____ Zip:_____

Gift Message: _____

Name: _____

Address: _____

City: _____ State:_____ Zip:_____

Gift Message: _____

Whisper'n Waters Order Blank

QTY		Price
	The Sacagawea Cookbook, $19.95 each	$
	The Lewis and Clark Cookbook, $19.95 each	$
	Art of the Lewis & Clark Trail , $42.95 each	$
	Add $3.95 *per order* for shipping and handling	$
	Sub Total	$
	ND Residents, add 6% sales tax	$
	TOTAL	$

Name: _____

Address: _____

City: _____ State:_____ Zip:_____

Telephone: _____ E-mail:_____

Credit Card/Acct. #: _____ Exp. Date:_____

Signature: _____

Send completed order form with payment to:

Whisper'n
WATERS

Whisper'n Waters, Inc.
328 Lunar Lane
Bismarck, ND 58503

VISA and MasterCard are welcome. Phone orders call: 1-888-282-7693 or fax: (701) 223-4259

Our cookbooks make a great gift for friends and family!

Gift orders mailed to:

Name:_____

Address: _____

City: _____ State:_____ Zip:_____

Gift Message: _____

Name:_____

Address: _____

City: _____ State:_____ Zip:_____

Gift Message: _____

Name:_____

Address: _____

City: _____ State:_____ Zip:_____

Gift Message: _____

Index

Epilogue

As she appeared so suddenly in our history, so she slipped into the misty ages of an ancient time. She was a sixteen-year-old mother, who walked half way across the continent and back with a group of armed men. The historians still debate what happened to her, as they should. It is important to read more than one historian's opinion. Most historians will agree one of her major contributions to the expedition was that of an "interpretress." Not only did she guide Lewis and Clark through understanding the similarities between the different cultures and themselves; but she also helped them appreciate their differences as well. We think she still is.

Jeffrey W. Evenson